# Maureen Kendal

D0237897

# Cyber
# and
# You

## The impact of technology on our lives

Legend Business Ltd, 107-111 Fleet Street, London, EC4A 2AB
info@legend-paperbooks.co.uk | www.legendpress.co.uk

Contents © Maureen Kendal 2019
The right of the above author to be identified as the author of this work has been asserted in accordance with the Copyright, Designs and Patents Act 1988. British Library Cataloguing in Publication Data available.

Print ISBN 9781789550078
Ebook ISBN 9781789550061
Set in Times. Printing managed by Jellyfish Solutions Ltd
Cover design by Tom Sanderson | www.the-parish.com

# CYBER AND YOU
# CONTENTS

# Introduction

Cyber is changing you: there is a huge impact of technology on our lives.
Cyber is changing: this impacts on you.
Cyber is everywhere: this changes your life.

Cyber is constantly evolving. It is not only technology that is impacting on us, but the way we live within our cyber world, positively using or abusing these enhancements. Internet Technology is pervasive. It permeates our lives, it is embedded in our homes and the products we buy, it determines our lifestyle. We are cyberselves. How we define our identity, our design choices, our relationships with family, friends and colleagues is usually linked to internet technology.

Technology permeates our politics. We face massive ruptures in political identities and affiliations. The means and might of influencing agents, such as: national states, international federations and unions and the media IT giants compete to dominate. The main global challenges are identified as climate change, global development and cyber awareness and cybersecurity. However, it is the complex inter-relationships between the actions that are taken to address these challenges which need to be recognised and investigated.

This book aims to explore areas of our lifestyle

that have changed and are evolving due to cyber technologies. It is crucial that we all are involved and help determine the future of cyber technology and the impact it is having on us, our social networks, identity and community and the global cyber landscape. If not, we could be walking blindfolded into disaster. We need to own the technological systems, not let the systems dictate to us.

# PART 1:
# THE CYBER LANDSCAPE

In the early-1990s, as we turned towards the 21st century, the internet, interactive multimedia and social media were perceived to be on the cutting edge. Since then we have been part of the transformational wave of social and cultural change. Today, culture, education, technological tools and communities are designed and delivered using digital production and distribution; offering the user a converged seamless digital cyber landscape. Smart systems and their tools – accessed via our smartphones – are used interchangeably for work and play, for pleasure and political advocacy. Smart technology is not only offering enablers for effective communication but also determining the quality of our relationships, our communities and lifestyles.

In 1999, I read, rather I consumed with excitement, 'The Age of Spiritual Machines', by Ray Kurzweil. I was seduced by the interweaving threads of the sci-fi episodic novel with knowledge about emerging internet technology. Kurzweil was concerned with anticipating how human relationships would change within the context of this new cyber world. Today Kurzweil continues to push the boundaries of emerging technologies and predicted the advent of cyberselves and beyond[1]. He advocates that transformational change and technological disruption, whilst transitioning every part of our lives, business, industry and society, is accelerating rapidly. This is an 'unprecedented period of transformational change'. He calls for the global agencies to develop 'an exponential mindset' to harness emerging technologies in order to 'create a better and more equitable future for us all'.

In 2008, Ray Kurzweil and associates supported the launch of Singularity University (SU)[2] at NASA Research Park in Silicon Valley. This academic institution aimed to bring together social values and emerging technologies to be a global catalyst for change. In 2018, the mission of SU continues to educate, empower, and inspire leaders to leverage exponential technologies to solve humanity's grand challenges[3]. The approach was iterative, dynamic, and multi-disciplinary with an emphasis on synthesis, convergence, and debate. Participants were from around the world, providing global input. The outcome is a global ecosystem of individuals and organisations who are inspired by SU's perspective and want to respond to SU's bold call-to-action. In order to grow, the business structure is set up to be a USA benefit corporation structure similar in tone to the UK's CIO and CIC business structures[4].

1. https://www.kurzweilai.net
2. singularity.org, https://su.org/about
3. https://su.org/blog/singularity-university-at-ten-years-the-early-days-evolution-to-benefit-corp/
4. CIO and CIC. A CIC is a type of company designed in particular for social enterprise that wants to use its profits and assets for public good. CICs are easy to set up and have all the flexibility of a company but with some special features to ensure they are working for the good of the community. CICs were developed out of the 2006 Charity Act and by 2013 there were over 8500 registered. CICs are subject to company law, have limited legal liability, paid directors and are subject to law as set out by Company House. . A CIO (Charitable Incorporated Organisation) is a charity that has to register with the Charity Commission even if it has income of less than £5000. It is subject to Charity Commission regulations. The all important difference between a CIO and an unincorporated charity is that the trustees will normally have limited or no liability and it can enter into contracts in its own right.

Exponentially accelerating technologies include cyber technologies. These emerging technologies offer significant advancements in artificial intelligence (AI), augmented reality (AR), virtual reality (VR), immersive reality (XR), data science, digital biology and biotech, medicine, nanotech and digital fabrication, networks and computing systems, robotics, and autonomous vehicles. Alongside these, global changes need to be addressed. Dynamic restless systemic relationships between different global challenges indicate a complex system. SU, in agreement with the World Economic Forum (WEF) postulate that the 'grand challenge of our time [is] to adapt to a world of accelerating change and apply technology for the greatest good.' SU's value-driven agenda sets out to solve 12 Global Grand Challenges (GGC): Resource Needs: Energy, Environment, Water, Food, Shelter, Space; *Societal Needs*: Security, Governance, Learning, Health, Disaster Resilience, Prosperity[5]. The tools we have to solve these challenges include cyber technology but crucially the capacity to work together, to share our thinking about change. Our mindset is changing. We, as part of our global system, will need to share conceptual frameworks. We need to build into these frameworks how to identify, define, monitor and evaluate inputs, outputs, outcomes, and impact. These methods, measures and the resulting outcomes need to be agreed through consensus and shared across different communities with different agendas. Designing with a shared mindset enables collaborative global decision-making. This process seeks to achieve measures of the common good, checks and balances within regulatory systems and how to generate, maintain and enforce codes of practice and law enforcement for the common good.

---

5. https://su.org/blog/singularity-university-at-ten-years-the-global-grand-challenges

We have started to think digitally. Peter Diamandis[6] articulated this journey of change as 6 Ds.

- Digitised – we are using computerised information science to manage our cyber lifestyles.
- Deceptive – we may hardly realise it is happening. It will be almost imperceptible.
- Disruptive – it will radically change our current lifestyles and systems making them obsolete.
- Dematerialised – things are becoming miniaturised, ubiquitous and pervasive, 'internet of things' known as IoT[7], everywhere, anytime.
- Demonetised – replicable and affordable through economics of scale.
- Democratised – accessible to all.

Technological change is exponential. In comparison to previous innovation, in the next century, we will not experience 100 years of progress, but 20,000 years. Ray Kurzweil has predicted that engineers will successfully reverse-engineer the human brain[8] by the mid-2020s. By the end of the 2020s, computers will be capable of human-level intelligence. Today, we are connected up to the internet, your social media channels and Google. By 2030, Ray Kurzweil believes that nano-robots will allow us to connect our biological nervous system to the cloud[9].

What 'human' values will we build into our computer systems and their decision-making?

---

6. https://su.org/concepts
7. The Internet of Things (IoT) includes all products and services which are internet enabled, for example, smart meters, smartphones, baby monitors, robotic toys, smart TVs and most cars are now smart with electronic updates. Everything that contains software as generally software needs to be updated via the internet and often connected to a home IT system.
8. https://www.livescience.com/33743-virtual-brain-henry-markram.html
9.https://singularityhub.com/2015/10/12/ray-kurzweils-wildest-prediction-nano-bots-will-plug-our-brains-into-the-web-by-the-2030s

We are in transition from embodied and physically enslaved homo sapiens into these new data-enhanced cyberselves. We may have thought of ourselves as 'innocent' homo sapiens, but with emerging universal access to the internet, all Earth citizens are being pushed out of this 'Garden of Eden'. Now we must take on the responsibilities of global challenges. When we vote for local politicians and councillors, often we focus on local challenges – we ask our politicians to ensure that our local councils fix the cracked pavements, police drug dealers on the street, prevent theft and violence, ensure the waste is regularly collected, ensure our local schools have enough places for local children. However, there are wider global systemic challenges at play and how do we play our part, stand up, be counted and contribute to the world as it accelerates exponentially into a new transition?

Local communities, for example, the Waorani communities in Ecuador use open source tools to collaboratively map their territory to defend their land rights[10]. Partnering with Digital Democracy[11] empowers marginalized communities to use technology to defend their rights and enable transformative change so that people can participate in decisions that govern their lives.

The new generation supporting Extinction Rebellion 'XR'[12] are gathering political leverage to combat global environmental challenges by using online communication channels to arrange gatherings and locations across geographically dispersed activists, but with physical back up in case the technology stops working or some agency pulls out broadband access.

10. In conversation with Talia Chain and Jessica Marie Knight, https://civichall.org/civicist/ecuador-waorani-communities-use-open-source-tools-collaborative-ly-map-territory
11. https://www.digital-democracy.org/aboutus
12. https://rebellion.earth

Recent actions included the backstop of bikers as messengers between activists. Cybertechnologies enable political power uprisings alongside the use of intermediate technologies, be they bikers or pigeon post or as in Egypt – video screening in the public town centre. 'XR' propose three demands to combat climate change. The third demand is the creation of citizens' assemblies that bring people together to learn, deliberate and make recommendations on an issue of public concern. If this is activated by government, online communication platforms could offer ways to engage popular citizen involvement to tackle environmental change[13]. Organisations like The RSA[14], SU[15] and WEF[16] offer common value-driven agendas to drive our new global society to design, develop and deliver new means to support this transitional journey.

How are we and our agencies preparing to address the challenges of disruption? In times of accelerated exponential surge in emerging technologies, there is the danger of throwing out traditional methods and excluding zones where we have felt comfort. This exclusion can have destructive ramifications. It is likely that we may not destroy everything, in order to 'reinvent the wheel', but rather consider practicable reforms rather than destructive revolutions. However, the legal framework and democratic processes need to be alive, responsive and somewhat dynamic and radical in order to serve the demands of their communities. Respecting benefits from traditional legacies and yet being able to nurture the capability to transform, points the way to a dynamic but delicately balanced and positive future.

Cyber technologies enable political power uprisings

13. In conversation with Talia Chain and Jessica Marie Knight, https://rebellion.earth/the-truth/demands/
14. The RSA, The Royal Society of Arts, Manufactures and Commerce. thersa.org
15. Singularity University, https://su.org
16. World Economic Forum, www.weforum.org

alongside the use of intermediate technologies, be they bikes or pigeons.

In *Beyond the Valley* (2019)[17], Ramesh Srinivasan asks: "As the digital takes over everything, whose voices matter?"[18] We are now in the advent of the Fourth Industrial Revolution; technologies are enabling global interconnectivity between products, environments, and communities. What is the transactional relationship that underpins the emerging technologies, internet and smart systems? Branded technology companies[19] enable uberization that offers services 24/7 when and where you need them, enables gig-jobs and the gig-economy, enables the collection of personal data – so that individuals become 'data products' as well as consumers. Tech giants collectively are worth more than most nation states. From his perspective in UCLA-University of California, Los Angeles, Silicon Valley, Ramesh Srinivasan calls to the American technology industry to go beyond their mindset, to encourage humanistic and democratic values within a diverse and multi-cultural world. His investigations into emerging technologies include smart systems which have been built using criteria that selectively recruit creating a gender and racial bias, worker re-skilling so people are re-trained to work with robotics and AI; worker cooperative schemes; building mesh-net[20] and community owned networks; opening up Africa by building up the communication network infrastructure to expand the internet; the Chinese One Belt One Road (OBOR) Initiative which for the last ten years has been

17. http://rameshsrinivasan.org/#about; http://digitalcultures.net
18. 2019, Ramesh Srinivasan, Beyond the Valley, MIT Press, Published November 1st, 2019.
19. For example: Apple, Amazon, Alphabet, Cisco, Facebook, IBM, Intel, Microsoft, Oracle, Tencent, Uber, Samsung and the technology companies who supply their components. https://www.toptenic.com/top-10-technology-companies/
20. http://www.mesh-net.org/portfolio/Anewinternetnotcontrolledbygovernment or tech giants. An alternative to the internet. Local networking technologies.

constructing an immense transportation infrastructure within which China invites the West to collaborate[21].

By 2017, OBOR the transportation highway was being realised across Asia, Europe, and northeastern Africa. OBOR will be coming somewhere near to you soon. The first train from China arrived in Barking, outer London, UK in 2017[22], the next step maybe into inner London, UK such as South Tottenham and Finsbury Park[23]. Physical transportation highways are embedded with smart systems and cyber communication networks. The OBOR 'concrete is already set' in Africa. Deep sea posts and harbours in the Baltic are being constructed[24]. The OBOR extends into Eastern Europe, Russia and Greece, competing with the Transatlantic Trade and Investment Partnership (TTIP). Currently, Trump is stimulating trade wars and has suspended TTIP as a trade agreement and alliance between the US and EU[25] [26]. Now, the US trades more with the EU than with China, but how will these trade markets be negotiated in the future? This political upheaval may leave an open door for China's ambition to develop an open trade tariff free eMarket in conjunction with the physical infrastructure of OBOR and integrated smart systems and cyber communication networks.

21. https://www.chinabusinessreview.com/one-belt-one-road-initiative-its-meaning-and-significance/

22. https://www.bbc.co.uk/news/uk-38666854

23. https://www.furtherfield.org. Dreamstudio.io in conversation with Digital Artists and Gallery agents, in 2017 at the Furtherfield Gallery, Finsbury Park. Discussion about possible futures that included trains from China to Finsbury Park, the impact of globalisation and artists working in virtual worlds, crypto-currency, the no tariff duty free global trade routes.

24. https://sputniknews.com/europe/201801111060666914-sweden-china-giant-harbor/

25. http://ec.europa.eu/trade/policy/in-focus/ttip/

26.https://www.thebalance.com/transatlantic-trade-and-investment-partnership-ttip-3305582; The Transatlantic Trade and Investment Partnership is a free trade agreement between United States and the EU. If completed, the TTIP would become the world's largest trade agreement. In 2017, President Trump suspended TTIP negotiations and is now engaging in a trade war.

# 1.1

# On becoming Cyborgs, Avatars, Transhuman and Cyberselves

Since just before the turn of this century, we have been witnessing ourselves as enhanced humans. We are enhanced in several ways: we are wired in, connected and networked into others; we are able to add our experiences through data uploads onto global networks of data collectors; we are able to sense beyond our physiology, i.e. access data from the wide electromagnetic radiation spectrum[27]; we are able to contribute and access global data feeds via search engines, i.e. Google. As enhanced humans, we are becoming cyborgs, avatars, transhuman[28] and cyberselves[29]. Entities connected to a global network, as contributors and users. Most of us carry smartphones or wearable computing products, a few have embedded digital systems as assistive technologies to tackle disabilities.

27. Sarwant Singh, with contributions from Lauren Taylor, Principal Consultant in Frost & Sullivan's Visionary Innovation Group (2017) https://www.forbes.com/sites/sarwantsingh/2017/11/20/transhumanism-and-the-future-of-humanity-seven-ways-the world-will-change-by-2030/#37cbd3337d79
28. https://imagine.gsfc.nasa.gov/science/toolbox/emspectrum1.html, accessed July 2019.
29. Sarwant Singh, ibid.

Since 1996, I have been using the internet and digital technology to design and produce digital media. Having started as a film-maker in the 1980s, my practice and my teaching career morphed into the industry of virtual immersive creative worlds. Most of us have experienced significant and radical changes in our work and life experience due to the impact of emerging technologies. Today, I design and develop virtual immersive experiences – and protect against cyber abuse. On one hand we create virtual worlds that reach out across communities to share and exchange ethics, resources and knowledge but on the other hand, we all need to tread with caution as this pervasive technology requires each of us to be protected against cyber abuse.

Cyber abuse is the result of destructive relationships whether in our personal relationships or in our wider relationships – be it as a consumer or producer in the commercial world or in our relationship as a citizen with our government. Abusive, toxic or dysfunctional relationships develop when traditional values and trust are eroded or under threat. Then ethical debate is required as a matter of urgency[30].

DreamStudio.io provides specialist services for artists and creators to enable design, production and user experience pipelines working with tangible media and digital worlds. Virtual avatar worlds, immersive technologies, augmented reality and similar technologies are at the forefront of how we are evolving to engage in these emerging platforms. The specifics of User

---

30. From a conversation between the author and Ruth Cigman, the philosopher. We need to address the new set of challenges to traditional values that are presented by the digital revolution. This is normally referred to today as ethical enquiry/ debate. Our contemporary multi-cultural multi-verse cannot sustain a unified, narrow perspective, but instead needs to work towards a shared, open, inclusive ethical framework.

Experience Design UX[31] for these immersive technologies are being developed. UX brings the users into the heart of design and delivery. Developers and UX specialists need to work with users/players of the technology and its platforms to innovate, play and experiment, to listen carefully to the interests, concerns and ambitions of users. Reaching out and collaboratively working with diverse groups of users, audiences and communities of interest will facilitate new ideas and prototypes for products and platforms. DreamStudio.io specialises in bringing together multi-disciplinary and diverse participants for focus groups and prototyping workshops, as well as archiving and curating artists' collections. To enable imaginative innovation, user needs and their playful experiments drive the project, whilst treating the type of technology platform as semi-agnostic. Technological platforms can be combined, merged and re-coded and/or blended with live opportunities to model and facilitate user journeys and experiences.

Today digital media tools are integrated within smartphones and laptops. Now media communication tools are not a specialist activity. Almost all citizens have media tools at their fingertips. In the future, digital media immersive tools will augment reality through a range of different forms of immersive experiences. Early adopters are exploring virtual, augmented and mixed realities. Researchers are identifying their benefits and constraints. Research stage pilots are now being phased into industrial developments, enabling users to try and test VR/AR/MR platforms.

Our lives are emerging into a new sense of self with tools that can augment our physical bodies, use our data to personalise services, share and manipulate our

---

31. User Experience Design UX, July 2019, https://www.interaction-design. org/literature/topics/ux-design. Insights and analysis of user experience. From conversations from ongoing projects with Mehmet Mulla, a UX specialist.

emotional narratives and memories. This transformation enables us to re-think societal values and philosophies. Whilst stone and bronze age people created early cave paintings evoking the physical realities of animals, people and landscapes they experienced, today our virtual worlds offer confined virtual caves and expansive open platforms. These immersive tools and environments will facilitate representations of our contemporary or retro-historical or imagined emotions, narrative journeys and experiences. The BBC dystopian drama, *Years and Years* (2019), includes a shockingly emotionally painful scene where the teenage daughter wearing an animated character head holographic enhancement, explains to her confused parents why she wants to become transhuman. The clip is titled 'I'm transhuman. I'm going to become digital'[32].

## DIGITAL CULTURE AND COMMUNITIES

Digital and virtual culture creates evocative and immersive experiences enabling people to become part of digital communities, to discover collections of narratives, objects and to explore and add to networks of knowledge.

There are many common community websites that we use every day such as Wikipedia and search engines like Google. As citizens, we use our local government website to apply for parking permits, to post an alert about rubbish dumping or problems in the neighbourhood. Sites like nextdoor.co.uk enable people in communities to exchange information on local crime incidents, sales of second hand goods and promote community and household services. We use government sites to register tax for vehicles, tax employment or to claim social benefits. As consumers,

32. Transhumanism. BBC Drama – Years and Years https://youtu.be/qOcktbXSfxU

more people are selecting and purchasing online for home delivery or to collect in store. As an employee, or volunteer, we need to go online to access essential information from our organisations. To access cultural, religious, community and social activities, we search, share, exchange, select and book online.

The penetration of smartphone ownership in the United Kingdom from 2013 to 2018, grouped by age, reported by Statista[33] indicates that in 2017, 95% of respondents aged between 16 and 24 reported owning a smartphone. What is shocking is the lack of mobile phone use in the over 55 year olds. Under 50% of over 55 year olds do not use or have a mobile phone! Who are the 5% who do not own a mobile phone in the over 16 year olds? How can citizens function effectively without internet access? Are these non-digital citizens using local libraries or good-natured friends and family to get online? One might ask why 5% of over 16 year olds and 40% of over 55 years olds are being excluded as digital citizens. Are they institutionalised, part of a religious sect that shuns technology, financially impoverished or have major learning difficulties? Gaps in citizens' online access need to be addressed.

## DIGITALLY RELUCTANT AND CAUTIOUS LATE ADOPTERS

I have met people who find the internet daunting. Let's identify this group as digitally reluctant and cautious late adopters. Friends, colleagues, clients or customers, they may not stay in this group forever, but they have been slowly passing through with a perception and attitude of unease about using digital technologies. I do understand how they must feel, sometimes I feel

---

33. Statista 2019, https://www.statista.com/statistics/271851/smartphone-own-ers-in-the-united-kingdom-uk-by-age/ Accessed 24 June 2019. The statistical trends are similar across Europe.

this unease – as the world rushes ahead – and we struggle to learn the latest platform, application or device interface. How can I make this damn phone or computer work? Many of us have been there. It is as if the world has changed so radically, without them or out of their control or without their consent. Some are either over 55, or have a disability such as deafness, are hard of hearing or have low disposable incomes or are just non-digital with defined moral principles or have special needs, or are fearful and scared of getting a smartphone and using online services. For them, using geo-location services, paying bills and household services online, internet usage, dealing with online documentation, connecting with their family and friends using text, email or social media, is becoming more challenging.

Cybercare UK[34] offers support to those who are victims and survivors of cyber abuse and cyber hacking. For individuals without technically-savvy support systems, Cybercare addresses these needs and offers introductory workshops to support cyber awareness, combat cyber abuse and the training to support the safe use of online devices. Cybercare offers problem-solving clinics and training workshops, customised for the needs of specialist groups including the digitally reluctant and cautious late adopters.

Below is a written witness statement, with the author's comments in brackets. This witness[35], Daniel, is recently retired, and now works part time supporting other disabled people. Daniel had been employed during his working adult life in government services, holds a university degree, has good practical skills and high intelligence. Daniel has been hard of hearing from

34. cybercare.org.uk, Since 2016, Cybercare in UK has advised and supported over 300 people and several organisations and service partners seeking helping with victims of cyber abuse.
35. Daniel, July 2019. Witness statement, verbal and written report to the author.

early childhood. Here he, as a witness, reports: "My experience with EE sales people in a high street retail outlets... my basic Mobi Wire mobile phone could no longer be topped up on a pay as you go basis via the HSBC ATMs. This service ended in May 2019. I thought arranging for a pay as you go contract would be a simple matter of getting a top up package... I duly went in person to the EE shop and a young salesman attended to me. He was young, tall and had a confident attitude. I explained that I am partially deaf with normal speech, and I wanted a top up contract with either advanced block placement or a pay as you go contract. He launched into a very fast and smooth sales pitch, and I only got key words and a gist of the sales pitch and patter. I was getting politely, inwardly flustered and less able to curb the long sales spiel. He asked if I had broadband. I in error must have given the impression that I did not have broadband. In a hair-breadth's moment, the salesman whipped out a Fibre Broadband optic fabric contract, I was putty in his hands. My instinct was to terminate this communication, as it was unbalanced." (The witness was bullied into signing the agreement). "I basically signed the contract, to get some vocal peace and assented to the agreement. Naturally I feel the fault was mine, and I should have never signed the contract. I should have been more in the negotiatory process, insisting on sentence breaks, so that I would have understood the depth and ramifications of the negotiations. What concerned me, with ample reflection on the sales pitch at the EE shop[36], was that when I queried anything, or tried to explain the need for understanding and the need for clearer speech, as a severely deaf person, they (the sales staff) either looked incredulous or just 'drilled' me. I think the roots of the communication issues are that the sales staff in

36. EE shop, a high street store which sells telecommunications packages for phones provided by EE.

their seeking of commercial products had not received deaf awareness training or forgot it." (Or choose to take advantage and bully this witness as a soft target.)

Daniel continues: "In general, the deeper malaise is that, in the modern technological aware younger generation, disabled people are not in their conscious lexicon or awareness. They are bombarded with images of a cyber-perfect world of beautiful people and lifestyles. The disabled are not invested or imbued with human qualities. They are out of mind, out of sight and negligible consumers with negligible earning potential. This attitude persists in the technology industry, as the technology sales people need to process complicated packages and terminology. They need to impress their peers." (And often sales people are financially rewarded to reach sales targets).

Technology providers may consider how best to train and reward their staff for providing appropriate support services for the disabled, elderly and other vulnerable sectors instead of pushing them to achieve sales from soft targets. Many consumers chose to buy online as the cheapest purchase option. Often these 'digitally cautious' customers need personalised and specialist support and therefore visit shops for face to face purchase and service advice.

Daniel, our witness came forward for support. After phoning EE and being directed to several different teams within EE, we were able, together, to put the case forward to EE for a mutually acceptable remedy. Through Cybercare, we have identified customers with disabilities or vulnerabilities who have not been supported to complain and without our support, may continue to be victims of these commercially targeted services.

## DIGITAL COMMUNITIES AS AN ENABLER AND AS A REGULATOR

Digital and virtual worlds can enable communication channels: to combat inequalities and war; to prevent global environmental disaster; to bring healthcare and education into remote or impoverished regions and to share and exchange culture, scientific know how and ethical values.

However, like all societies, the digital world is subjected to exploitation, greed and abuse. To combat Cybercrime, the cyber world needs regulation, monitoring and enforcement. Protecting the cyber world, needs technical and effective monitoring across several layers of communication technology networks. A global legal regulatory framework and effective legal enforcement needs to be implemented. An ethical code of practice is required to underpin all education services with consideration of global, national, regional and local perspectives. Checks and balances to ensure personal liberty, freedom of speech are crucial. How can global regulatory structures ensure justice and compassion, personal liberty to speak out but not to endanger others? The battle for liberty may mask abuse and exploitation of the vulnerable. The tightening of regulation may produce overpowering state control and fascism. We walk delicately on a narrow bridge between regulation and freedom. Yet, it is understood that we live in a time of less war, abuse and violence than ever before.

## ENTROPY, PERCEPTION OF 'CHAOS' AND THE ILLUSION OF THE 'CURE'

There is a perpetual return from our perception of civilisation to one of perceived chaos. A metaphor for this is a common garden; we mow the lawn, beheading the daisies, a month later, the manicured lawn is a diversity of grasses and wild flowers – a return to a wilderness. Should we be frightened of a dystopian tendency where our 'civilised' society returns to a lawless chaotic anarchy?

Steven Pinker[37] puts forward a sound case for reason, science, humanism and progress[38]. However, we need to be careful on how we understand science and probabilistic thinking, what factors are being measured and how. There is a need for us all to be educated to understand science, computing and our smart systems. We, as cyber-individuals, families and communities, need to influence and determine the cyber system, rather than cyber systems being in control of us. How we chose to regulate our digital communities needs to be explored. We need to ask questions to investigate who is using what, why and the outcomes. We need to design frameworks for online and 'blended'[39] systems that need to be tested and iteratively developed to benefit its users and stakeholders, and to protect and support any disadvantaged user groups.

We may seek to evaluate progress in terms of happiness. In the developed world, humans might be perceived as fattened domesticated complacent creatures, over-dosed by media feeds and seduced by a succession of branded products. A simplistic approach to evaluate success often only measures happiness and socio economic relative wealth. Happiness is more likely to be evident where individuals are enabled to be in control of their lives and lifestyle decisions,

37. Steven Pinker, Enlightenment Now, 2018, Viking.
38. ibid
39. 'Blended' communities and services use both online-virtual and physical communication using an integrated model. This works well, where the conceptual framework and reference points for both online-virtual and physical 'face to face, body to body' environments are integrated, common and shared.

where individuals are enabled to problem-solve, to meaningfully contribute to their communities and live creative lives.

As Pinker (2018)[40] notes, the nature of the world is entropic, in a sense, 'naturally' directing itself towards a world of chaos and uncertainty, or randomness. I would add that this is a perception, noting that our perceptions of chaos can be mathematically modelled, and attributed to biological and geographical tendencies of species distribution, dominance, regression and extinction. However, given the assumption of an entropic world, we can always be certain that there will be problems to solve and that our biological disposition will enable us to anticipate, to fear and feel anxiety, in moderation, and this will motivate our problem-solving and creativity. Along this line of thought, we can never reach 'paradise', or achieve a static balance, or find the ultimate 'cure'. The best approach requires societal systems that enable dynamic iterative adaptation.

As a young person in the 1970s and early 1980s, I journeyed through 'finding myself' through exploring identity and the nature of self. Could we ever feel as if we were a 'unified self'? I had always felt a sense of being a fragmented or divided self, assembling a sense of order out of a fast changing chaotic rotating world. Like many others, I had migrated from another country to the UK, and have a sense of being from neither one place nor another, always feeling on the edge of any culture or group. I was fortunate enough to have had deep and stable early attachments within the family, despite an evolving and sometimes threatening world outside.

At that time, I pursued Psychology, and during 1980-1983, I was a research assistant to Dr David Malan[41] and his team at the Tavistock Clinic, carrying

40. Steven Pinker, Enlightenment Now, 2018, Viking.
41. Malan, D.H. (1979). Individual Psychotherapy and the Science of Psychodynamics London: Butterworth-Heinemann.

out a longitudinal study on the effect of brief dynamic psychotherapy on a large group of patients and whether these therapeutic interventions could achieve the outcome of 'the cure'. The concept of psychological recovery and the 'cure' were derived from psychoanalytic and cognitive research. To determine if a patient had been cured, four trained therapists assessed long term stable committed relationships and employment. Something did not ring true for me in that these traditional measures of the 'cure' did not match entirely my observations. I had seen people in psychological distress acting out, creatively working through, accommodating to their environments and becoming functional. I had experienced and observed a capacity to develop functional attachment, ability to tolerate separation and loss, and thus a respect for difference; then developing the capacity to mature a sense of self and established social connectedness.

Today, in tune with changing societal expectations, the 'cure' is not measured solely with these traditional expectations. Today therapeutic interventions facilitate a fluid and continual adjustment and a creative and dynamic understanding of who we are. Through our own acknowledgement and recognition of our early attachment experiences, how we ourselves deal with anxieties, fears, projected defences and resistance. Given this psychological recognition, we contribute positively to society. Whilst the psychological developmental journey may be supported through a therapeutic intervention and/or interpretation, the crucial factor is that this is a journey actively undertaken by the individual with a sense of integrity. This capacity to creatively establish a sense of self, today takes place in part within cyberspace, in a space which integrates the cyber and the real world. We are using social media platforms to develop our sense of our cyberself.

## UNDERESTIMATING THE NEED FOR RAPPORT, PHYSICAL EMBODIMENT AND EMPATHY

As in all areas of our lives, the online experience needs to be integrated with the real human need to connect, of being heard and the capacity to listen. Experience as a cyberself may augment our lives, but it may not necessarily offer a complete experience of self. We can specify and 'code in' our lifestyle choices on digital virtual platforms and services. The crucial question is where do we need 'the human physical touch' and what can be scaffolded into an online system. Brief dynamic psychotherapy has evolved, offering a scaffolded online therapeutic intervention[42]. Johansson et al.'s research (2013), indicate that psychodynamic treatment approaches may be transferred to the guided self-help format and delivered via the Internet. However one of the seminal insights from research in the early-1980s indicated that the crucial factor of being able to establish rapport with the psychotherapist was of greater significance than the specific type of psychotherapy training that had been undertaken by the therapist. We underestimate the need to establish rapport with another human, virtual or physical, at our peril.

If I consider all my experiences in the virtual worlds – designing and developing online virtual parks, avatar worlds, immersive VR environments – I have observed and experienced first-hand that we have the capacity to establish a level of rapport with others within a virtual world. However, the depth and commitment to these relationships are significantly more developed within a blended context. Robin Dunbar's research[43] reinforces

42. Johansson, R., Björklund, M., Hornborg, C., Karlsson, S., Hesser, H., Ljótsson, B., Rousseau, A., Frederick, R.J. & Andersson, G. (2013). Affect-focused psychodynamic psychotherapy for depression and anxiety through the Internet.
43. Robin Dunbar – https://www.psy.ox.ac.uk/team/robin-dunbar. Further research indicates: Cross-cultural similarity in relationship-specific social touching, Suvilehto, JT. et al, (2019), Proc Biol Sci, 286

that observation. Families, friendships, communities and significant emotional relationships can and do take place online. We might text, WhatsApp, or video each other even when we are in the same house or room! Skin to skin contact is crucial for mothers and babies[44], and for all of human development, our emotional well-being and lifestyle. We are mammalian animals[45], whether enhanced and mediated by cyber technologies or not. Again, we underestimate the need for physical embodied contact with another human, virtual or physical, at our peril.

Addressing this need and paving the way for online robotic systems and perhaps online avatars to offer an effective touch sense function, a team of scientists led by Professor Tee recently invented Asynchronous Coded Electronic Skin (ACES) that offers ultra-high responsiveness and robustness to damage and can be paired with any kind of sensor skin layers to function effectively as an electronic skin. ACES differs from previous current electronic skins which are sensitive to damage and difficult to scale up[46].

Today, all our lifestyle processes are being managed by smart systems which embed AI feedback loops, picking up our data – feeding forward these past data patterns, enabling the system to predict back to us recommended routes forward to guide our future actions. Soon we become reliant on the efficacy of the smart system, but whose values will the smart system be serving? If the online world with its smart system

44. https://www.unicef.org.uk/babyfriendly/baby-friendly-resources/implementing-standards-resources/skin-to-skin-contact/ accessed July 2019.
45. Human as mammalian animals have a highly developed sense of touch.
46. Professor Benjamin Tee and his team from National University of Singapore, Materials Science and Engineering (2019). Asynchronous Coded Electronic Skin (ACES): A neuro-inspired artificial peripheral nervous system for scalable electronic skins. Science Robotics; 17 Jul 2019; Vol. 4, Issue 32, eaax2198; DOI: 10.1126/scirobotics.aax2198;
https://robotics.sciencemag.org/content/4/32/eaax2198

serves the requirements, let us say, of the majority, or what is understood to be the 'common good', what about the individual who may not fit in? Again, we underestimate the need to include the Other within our tribal groupings, virtual or physical, at our peril.

Outraged about happenings within the social media community world, a second witness, Simone, an advocate for disability rights and changing perspectives[47], discussed with the author the use of her experience on online channels. Whilst social media community groups can enable self help and advocacy communities, they can also self-regulate, ex-communicate and block users in order to regulate and socially control attitudes, thereby excluding people that do not share their views. A special needs or disadvantaged group is not necessarily more tolerant and empathetic than other social groups.

Our witnesses, Simone, Daniel and others, also reflected on how sometimes special needs communities can be inward looking, insular and do not allow different opinions within their own online social media groups. Many groups have a self-regulating function, throwing out participants who have an alternative view or approach. Who holds the power as organiser of the group? Who is enabled to be moderator? What are the guidelines and social conventions for what is understood to be appropriate use of language, meaning and 'allowed' topics? How are these guidelines developed and communicated? When we advocate liberty of expression, we need to be able to understand the effect that speech and media expressions can have within the context of not moderated or inappropriately moderated social media and communication channels.

47. From a conversation with Simone, July 2019 – A campaign manager for ALLFIE, The Alliance for Inclusive Education. The organisation believes in the right of all disabled learners to access and be supported in mainstream education. https://www.allfie.org.uk

Promoting liberty and the right of freedom of speech may not protect a minority's right to be protected from speech that is understood by them to be disrespectful and abusive[48]. The infamous Charlie Hebdo satirical online and printed magazine brought this tension to public debate in 2015, after a terror attack in response to a cartoon of a religious prophet, followed by further arrests and investigations in December 2018[49]. At the time, I was asked, in fact, bullied, to express a point of view on this debate. I did not, but what I did say was that 'we' need to listen, to listen carefully and sensitively to all of the stake-holders, get the communities of interest around a table. Comedy and satire are an essential part of the 'commentaria'[50] of an enlightened society. Freedom of speech is the cornerstone of liberty. However, respect, empathy and compassionate understanding are essential partners that need to accompany access to these 'trees of knowledge'; today these are multitudinous eddies of media, communication and information.

---

48. Charlie Hebdo – Satirical magazine, secular, political and jubilant, out every week on newsstands and every day on the internet. https://charliehebdo.fr/en/
49. A French terror suspect linked by police to the 2015 attack on Charlie Hebdo that killed 12 people has been arrested in Djibouti. Peter Cherif, 36, also known as Abou Hamza, is to be transferred to France for questioning over allegations he masterminded the shootings in Paris at the satirical newspaper. Peter/Abou was a close friend of brothers Chérif and Saïd Kouachi, who burst into Charlie Hebdo's office on 7 January 2015 and gunned down staff at an editorial conference. The brothers escaped, killing a police officer on the way out, and fled north. They died in a shootout at a print-works two days later. The attack came after the newspaper carried satirical depictions of a religious prophet on its front page. Reported December 2018, accessed July 2019.
50. 'Commentaria': this is not 'Commentariat', which is defined as a group of powerful and influential commentators, rather I am defining 'Commentaria' as the capability in many cultures and civilisations of enabling persons from unique diverse socio-historical perspectives to comment and intellectually argue freely but hopefully with compassionate sensitivity, from another's point of view, focussing on a specific challenge. Over time, this enables the building up of layers of diverse opinions and responses. For example: Responsa commentaries as an example of a development of literary and legal discussion and debate. https://www.responsa.co.il

Every day we are seduced by illusions, superstitions, prejudices, fake news inherent in advertising and media, by ideologies within religion, politics and economic agendas, seductively drip feeding temptations onto our screens and channels. Is something true because many people buy into it? Gambling and astrological charts are both 'economic goods'. So, as a business 'good' they exist. That is true. People do purchase these astrological stories, people do purchase gambling experiences and thus these have value as a business transaction. Do you believe in horoscopes and astrological predictions? If so, why are we seduced? Why are gamblers convinced that one day they will win? The objective reality is the only long term winner is the gambling business owner. Why do we believe what we see/hear/read online?

Are we educated to 'read' media and knowledge accessed online, to understand it with discernment, with tools of analysis? Following traditions of analytical learning within cultures, which encourage 'commentaria'[51], are we enabled to discuss, debate, analyse and question? What are our tools of investigation and enquiry?[52] Do online forums for debate fulfil their purpose? What rules are these moderators directed by, and for whose benefit?

Online moderation is not new. Fifteen years ago, one of my children joined a teenage/young adults readers' forum set up by a well-known children's author. The forum enabled a community of readers to develop their appreciation of literature and to develop their own writing by using a 'game' with a tag-team. On this online platform, readers could collaboratively write stories with other readers geographically dispersed. One reader started to discuss the political conflicts in the Middle East. Immediately, the moderator flagged

51. ibid
52. In conversation with Imogen, a psychology student at Sussex University. July 2019

this up and issued a warning indicating that this was inappropriate material for this online forum. On one hand, this censorship restricted freedom of thought, speech and creativity, prohibiting these young adults being able to discuss and debate openly. There may have been issues that they felt strongly about and/or were facing within the context of their lives; on the other hand these controls kept the online forum safe from any repercussions that may have occurred by discussing these controversial issues openly and therefore allowed young adults in many 'closed' countries to develop creative writing and communication skills. Without this control, the online forum may have been closed down by national authorities who were bound by strict political censorship. Any online community has a range of stakeholders that require consideration. The needs of the individual, social groups, communities, legal protection, business interests, national interests and security need to be finely balanced. The online world is globally accessed. Never before has the need for international codes of practice and standards been so crucial. Societies aim to protect their citizens using commonly shared educational ethical guidelines and standards, backed up by government and legal enforcement agencies. Yet our online world is challenged. Our reality offers a multi-verse of diverse ideas with tolerance and respect for the Other. There is a hope that these ideals of liberalism will continue to develop into the emerging online world. This fine tuning, of how best to balance freedom and control within the global landscape, is being played out.

**DIGITAL COMMUNITIES**

Digital communities are here to stay – they offer inter-connectivity and ease of communication 24/7, enabling us to move and act freely and faster than ever before. They can support the downfall of unethical regimes. Within the everyday context of our communities and families, they frequently enable technical support across groups. Often within families, informal inter-generational knowledge-sharing includes grandparents relying on grandchildren to set up their devices and support online transactions.

Digital communities like the Digital Collections, Discovering Communities (DCDC) and TED, have been developed within creative and cultural industries, enabling ideas and collections to become globally connected and reach out to new audiences and distant locations. Since 2013, the DCDC conference has brought together participants from creative and cultural industries, museums, galleries, public education experiences and emerging technology platforms. In 2019, the DCDC conference focuses on navigating the digital shift: practices and possibilities, developers and suppliers[53]. The TED Talks[54] offer an online platform to spread ideas, creativity, inspiration, to benefit people. TED is a nonpartisan nonprofit community which hosts short, powerful talks. 'TED began in 1984 as a conference where Technology, Entertainment and Design converged, and today covers almost all topics – from science to business to global issues – in more than 110 languages.'[55]

Digital Communities are often influencers or followers of the 'Tech for Good' trend, distinguishing themselves from organisations which use emerging technology just for financial profit or economic power. The Tech for Good[56] movement encourages the development of

53. The DCDC (Digital Collections, Discovering Communities) conference, 2019. https://dcdcconference.com
54. https://www.ted.com/talks
55. https://www.ted.com
56. Tech for Good, https://www.meetup.com/techforgood

applications that seek to make a difference to the most urgent world challenges. The RSA offers a competition to showcase Tech for Good organisations[57]. Some online smart projects re-distribute food to the needy; others teach computer coding and IT to vulnerable and uneducated groups of people who are living in geographically dispersed regions. For example, the 'Digital skills for today' programme and its networks enable IT and coding training for youth, including young women, in areas suffering from conflict and unrest in North Africa and Middle East. This enables the youth to develop long term employment opportunities, digital innovation and entrepreneurship in marginalised communities[58].

There is a significant trend where smart systems are developed to improve medical research and practice. Smart applications allow the user to access, through smart phones and smart watches, medical and physiological monitoring; other applications enhance medical supplies, or patient care, or alert medics to specific patient need.

Example one: A memorable project is Zipline, carrying blood and medical supplies using drone technology in Rwanda and Ghana[59]. Their mission statement is to provide every human on Earth with instant access to vital medical supplies. They have built the world's fastest and most reliable delivery drone, the world's largest autonomous logistics network, and they have invested in a highly engaged and active team.

Example two: Research centres like the UK Dementia Research Institute Care Research & Technology at

57. The RSA. https://www.thersa.org/action-and-research/rsa-projects/
economy-enterprise-manufacturing-folder/future-work-awards/winners
58. https://digitalskillsfortoday.org
https://flyzipline.com
59. https://techcrunch.com/2019/04/24/drone-delivery-startup-zipline-launch-es-uav-medical-program-in-ghana/

Imperial[60] are using new technologies to tackle the increasing challenge of dementia in the elderly, developing new technologies to create dementia-friendly 'Healthy Homes' and provide insights into how dementia develops.

Example three: Google division DeepMind has developed an AI tool that could predict acute kidney injury (AKI) up to 48 hours in advance. DeepMind also unveiled results from research conducted by the University College London of its mobile medical assistant for clinicians called Streams. The Royal Free London NHS Foundation Trust has been using the app since early-2017. Streams leverages the current national AKI algorithm in the UK to notify on patient deterioration. At the NHS Trust, Streams has been reported to save up to two hours per day for clinicians. Google plans to absorb DeepMind's health technology unit, and its Streams app team, into its health subsidiary, Google Health[61].

The waves of emerging organisations, innovation hubs within tech giants and new start-up companies aim to use technology to encourage social good with value-driven agendas. Within this wave, a small start-up, Cybercare Ltd and Cybercare Trust are developing technology solutions to enable its workforce to effectively support individuals, families and communities who are combating cyber abuse. Cyber intrusion can occur across different points of risk and vulnerability within our IT lifestyle, as we work, play and socialise, on the move or at home. Criminal activity to undermine secure cyber communications is one of the biggest global challenges – alongside political conflict and environmental threats.

60. https://ukdri.ac.uk/news-and-events/uk-dri-care-research-technology-at-imperial
61. https://www.medicaldevice-network.com/digital-disruption/deepmind-ai-kidney-injury

# 1.2

# Cyber-Mind, The Self as Code, CyberSects, The Selfie and the Other.

' *...although not born-digital, (humans) are recreating themselves as coded objects imbued with a digital identity and living on the internet with a URL address integrating with billions of data bits, as their coded life flows seamlessly across the digital eco-system.*' Bowen and Giannini, 2019[62].

This is an apt description of our human identity today. However, do we feel different to the human being that we were in the pre-Internet 20th century era? Digital technology is enabling us to speed up, link up and action complex functions in line with the exponential increase of super computer systems. Our interactions and lifestyle are now so fast, in response there is a parallel call for an increase in mindfulness, the need for a different pace, a slowing down to enable reflection and meditation, allowing space for us to consider the

---

62. Digital Art, Culture and Heritage: New constructs and consciousness, Jonathan P. Bowen, Tula Giannnini, Rachel Ara, Andy Lomas and Judith Siefring, EVA 2019.

consequences before we act. This increased awareness is playing a part in our cyberworld. Screen-time alerts enable us to monitor the balance of screen time versus face-to-face contact with real humans and real physical environments.

Today digital and virtual artist-technologists and their communities are exploring beyond 'mindfulness', states of perception and consciousness. They pay homage to several legacies mind-enhancing culture, religious and spiritual traditions, and emerging counter-culture initiatives.

These legacies included mind expanding drug culture, from pagan, religious and Rastafari rites, the poet Coleridge and to the 1960s experiments of Timothy Francis Leary, Carlos Castaneda and Aldous Leonard Huxley and then religious and spiritual traditions that formed part of the New Age 1960s meditation movements including Maharishi Mahesh Yogi (1918-2008) an Indian guru, known for developing the Transcendental Meditation technique. Then counter-culture influencers like Buckminster Fuller and EF Schumacher.

Immersive communities[63] are developing new states of perception and consciousness enabled by cyber technologies and triggered by experiences within and across immersed spaces. This interest in the development of transhumanism and new states of consciousness is explored by researchers and organisations. Technology enables us as humans, as cyberselves, to experience beyond initial materiality into other perceptual and conceptual spaces. Examples of these types of explorations are led by Professor Carl Smith of the Learning Technology Research Centre (LTRC), at Ravensbourne University. Other networks include Decoded Futures events[64]. Digital empowerment is about gaining

---

63. https://www.projectimmersed.org/london; https://www.immerseuk.org
64. https://www.stylus.com/summits

exposure to skills, technologies and experiences. A Digital Skills Academy, decoded.com, promotes their programmes as ways of 'democratising data'.

Despite the technical online interconnectivity, people can suffer from a sense of disconnectedness and a lack of real connection with other humans[65]. There is a thirst for a return to something, some values which are beyond our everyday experiences. For some, these might be a yearning for 'spiritual' or nationalistic or religious values. However, for many, this thirst evokes a return to a value driven agenda, a recognition of our humanness, our need for supportive relationships, ethical purpose, moral values, nurturing communities and a need to rescue the Earth from ecological challenges. Sometimes this evolves into a quest to create spiritual, creative and ecological communities integrated with an online presence. The ease of access to cyber communication channels is often embraced by many to reach out to and participate in their chosen communities, integrating online and real world experiences.

Meanwhile for others – this evokes a return to the superstitious or even a fascistic form of fundamentalism or nationalism, alongside which state ideological, traditional mainstream and orthodox religious groups are facing challenges from cyber-sects. Online communication channels facilitate and enable user interactivity and peer to peer information sharing, thus enabling new cults and groupings. These cyber-sects can easily offer alternative belief systems and undermine widely held and entrenched sets of ideas and traditional moral directives. Current examples of cyber-attack on different religious and political sects are evident in China, Muslim and the Christian world, and across many political

---

65. In conversation with Jessica Marie Knight, writer and artist, currently Artist in Residence at Sadeh Farm, July 2019, https://sadehfarm.co.uk/artist-residency-space

divisions. 'Cybersect' now loosely refers to any people online (cyborgs or cybernauts) with a collaborative agenda using the Internet for text distribution, recruitment, and information sharing. In fact, most of us, when we are online, are part of several cyber communities that support our local, religious, sports, cultural or educational engagement. Online communities offer the opportunity of distributing information peer-to-peer, many-to-many, rather than the one-to-many traditional hierarchical model.

On online social media and video channels, charismatic leaders, opinion leaders, bloggers and TED talk leaders have built significant crowds of followers, emulating the one-to-many/leader-follower model. Hive or herd instincts are reborn. As followers or 'friends' we follow and comment on each other's walls and channels. Many people participate in the twittering channels – creating a cacophony of sound bites – seemingly as prolific as birdsong. Humans are social animals, enjoying the sharing of enthusiasms, passions, political rallies, sport matches or cultural events. We engage both online and physically in real space. The online and the physical tangible experience both reinforce and also contradict each other. There is pervasive osmotic seepage between the virtual and the real. We are here in our own physical space and over there, elsewhere, 24 hours a day, 7 days a week, co-existing in multiple universes.

Given all this interconnectedness, some people are still lonely and feel disconnected. Some people are addicted to their online experiences – their social media or gaming as if the internet were an opiate-fuelled pleasure dome. Other people search to escape from this chattering online world. Online experience can exacerbate feelings of loneliness, disconnection, addiction and a yearning to escape from its clutches. But for most of the time, many of us live with its benefits, whilst recognising the need to moderate our usage and achieve a healthy balance between our online lifestyle and our physical tactile world. Thus, we are enabling an integration of our cyberselves and our identities.

## CYBER-ROBOTIC SELVES, THE UNCANNY VALLEY, DAEMONS, COMPANION ROBOTS

'Uncanny Valley' was coined by Masahiro Mori in 1970, describing our strange revulsion toward things that appear nearly human, but somehow *not quite right*. This revulsion is a reaction towards electronically mediated simulations and robots designed to simulate humans, but also can include virtual or augmented reality experiences, computer animations and medical re-constructions of human-like enhancements. This use of the uncanny builds on Freud's use of 'unheimleich'[66], and our repressed fear of 'death' and/or the Other.

Some postulate that the Uncanny Valley sensation is created by the perception of simulated electronic visualisation experiences or humanoid like robots. This experience feels to us, almost like our real experience but not quite.

Some call this sensation a pathogen avoidance, however, it may rather be an instinct which seeks to avoid 'difference', rather than assimilate evolutionary predators. This complex relationship of avoidance and/ or assimilation is maybe similar to the dominance of Homo Sapiens that occurred over millions of years when Neanderthals became extinct or were assimilated into the new human species.

An additional instinct might be that humanoid-like

66. unheimlich – this is not merely unhomely, but refers to Freud's belief that what we find the most eerie or scary originates not from the exotic or foreign, but from what was originally familiar then repressed and subsequently remanifested in an uncanny/unheimlich guise.

robots today look like life-less puppets. Some suggest that the image of a life-less puppet or a robotic doll that can be turned off might trigger a fear of death and mortality. However, our rich multi-cultural story-telling legacies identify many artificially created human-like creatures, often created to respond to a need or request by the human hero.

Ancient and contemporary myths, legends and stories portray characters who are created out of dust, clay, magic, mechanics or electronics. Often they become or seem to become alive, pointing to a moral sense of what it means to be fully human and take on human responsibilities in situations of loss and fear of death. These artificially created characters have an uncanny power to unsettle their audiences and also to inspire many re-makes, re-creating new versions of uncanny human-like replicas, across generations.

- **Coppélia** or The Girl with the Enamel Eyes is the mechanical puppet doll in the Ballet of Coppella, first performed in 1870. The seemingly animated live-puppet girl is created by a lonely puppet-maker[67].
- **Frankenstein** or The Modern Prometheus by Mary Shelley, first published in 1818, tells the story of Victor Frankenstein, a young scientist who creates a hideous, sapient creature in a scientific experiment. The novel draws on the author's psychological feelings of loss following the deaths of loved ones. In a sense the creation of the monster could be understood as a creative response to those irreplaceable losses. Furthermore, capacity to create can be motivated by a desire to recreate a feeling of memory, of loss, of the shadow, reflection

67. https://www.roh.org.uk/showings/coppelia-live-2019

or after-effect of a deep emotional bond with another person, community or the sensation of an early childhood garden.

- **The Golem** is an animated anthropomorphic being that is magically created entirely from inanimate matter (usually clay or mud)[68]. The word was used to mean an amorphous, unformed material, taken from the Psalms (approximately 1000BCE) and developed in medieval writing. Judah Loew ben Bezalel, known as the Maharal, a rabbi of Prague (1520-1609) brought the Golem to life to defend the Prague ghetto from anti-Semitic attacks and pogroms.
- **The Body of Glass** (UK title) or 'She and IT' by Marge Piercy (US title) 1991, tells the futuristic story of Shira, a woman who has a relationship with Yod, an illegal male cyborg (described as full AI in a human shaped vehicle).
- **His Dark Materials** by Philip Pullman (1995) portrays characters who have personal and attached daemons[69]. 'Northern Lights' and 'The Golden Compass' , tell of the adventures of an 11-year-old, Lyra Belacqua, and her dæmon, Pantalaimon. Pullman's dæmons sit on the shoulders of the characters, appearing and disappearing, as if activated or triggered by need (part conscience, commentary, a witch's familiar), and I would suggest uncannily similar to a virtual AI assistant.

Today, in the UK, instead of those imaginary sci-fi robots who were built to look like humans, our focus has been to develop robotic assistants and guides

---

68. Jewish Scriptures, Psalm 139.
69. Greek mythology describes daemons as benign nature spirits, later Plato understands them as intelligent assistants to each human soul.

that are integrated or attached to human agents, for example, our cyberselves with our smartphones, drone robots that fly, nano-robots that are microscopic and AI self-learning autonomous components within our smart systems.

However, humanoid-looking robots like Pepper[70] have been caring for the elderly in Japan[71] and are now available in the UK. Robotic pets are being distributed to alleviate loneliness in the elderly and in addition researchers are investigating if 'smart' pets could be especially helpful to individuals with mild dementia[72]. Robots of London provide a range of robots for hire and sale[73].

Today those who are reluctant to go digital will either become extinct or get partially assimilated into the main stream of digitally enhanced cyberselves. We are a new species – networked, digital, conscious of others, of data, of trends, like never before. Each of us is attached, as it were, to our smart online system through our smartphone, laptop, digital watch and other Internet-enabled devices known as IoT, and to global data and information systems and some now have companion humanoid or animal-like robots.

Similarly to our cultural history of stories with their seemingly artificial human-like creatures, we seek services from our digital assistant, our smartphones. We seek services that might fill gaps of loneliness, to reclaim photographic memories, to recall past feelings and relationships, to find people with similar interests, or people that belong to our tribe with shared values and ideas. We may need to seek protection from attack or intelligence and knowledge about events and people

70. https://www.techinasia.com/smiby-robot-baby-for-japan-elderly
71. Replacing Humans | Robots Among Us in Japan,
https://www.youtube.com/watch?v=dbO8JRqlIWU
72. https://www.healthline.com/health-news/how-robotic-pets-can-help-sen-iors-with-loneliness#1
73. https://www.robotsoflondon.co.uk/pepper

that are not immediately obvious, covert or hidden. Our dæmons or Digital Assistants with their use of AI share and exchange previously hidden intelligence and expose this knowledge to us. They are designed to protect us, to seek the best options and pathways on our behalf. Within this context, these dæmons are created to be our guardian angels. It is crucial that we understand when to believe them and take their guidance and when not to. It is crucial that we are in control and take responsibility. We cannot blame 'the gremlin in the machine'[74]. We are collectively the system's designers, developers, distributors, as well as its users and players. We, as users and players, need to understand and act to configure our cyber systems correctly in order to enable them to keep us safe.

## DIGITAL ASSISTANTS: ALEXA, SIRI, CORTANA, ASSISTANT AS INDUSTRY COMPETITORS

Will the digital assistant reflect and mirror our requirements or interfere with our autonomy and freedoms? The main function of today's digital assistants is to respond to human voice commands to help the user achieve a task. They guide the user and can be coded to control functions. Do they always work? Are they safe? How much control should we, as users retain? When and how much should we rely on their guidance? Does your GPS[75] navigation app – be it

74. 'The gremlin in the machine.' At the start of my journey working with computerised multi-media systems, a university tutor, would explain away my questions as, 'It must be a gremlin in the machine'. I would imagine an image of a gremlin and laugh as I rebooted the computer. However, as a creative problem-solver, who was born with insatiable curiosity, asking 'why', time and time again, I chose to explore what the gremlin in the system actually was and root it out. Not always serving any external interests, who might plead: 'Let sleeping dogs lie'.
75. Global Positioning System (GPS), originally NAVSTAR GPS, is a satellite-based radio navigation system owned by the United States government and operated

Apple Maps, Google Maps or Waze[76], – always find the best route, or are you led up a mountain path or into a field, or new building area with a different road layout?

Digital assistants have had immediate appeal to early adopters, technically interested consumers but also have useful functions for the elderly, and less physically able – providing functions that can be physically challenging thereby offering comfort, versatility and independence.

Voice search statistics released in 2019[77] indicate 30-60% of people are using voice search functions offered by digital assistants. I have a weekly scheduled phone call meeting with an Apple user who calls in using Siri to activate his phone-call during his urban commute. However, I get this uncanny feeling when I, as a bystander, am forced to hear another commuter's conversations to their dis-embodied person in conversation with them. Hypocritically, I choose to sit in a quiet coach for any city to city long distance travel to avoid the audio disruption of this type of audio distraction. The uncanny sensation comes from on one hand the curiosity of audio voyeurism and on the other a desire to retain the audio privacy of our own spaces and thoughts. Yet our digital assistants are here to stay, embedded and embodied, integrated in our wearable computing, maybe within our contact lenses or even under our skins, not unlike Phillip Pullman's daemons as if 'perched on our shoulders'[78].

There is a choice of Digital Assistants designed and delivered by different online corporates: Apple delivers Siri;

by the United States Air Force, which provides geolocation and time information to a GPS receiver anywhere on or near the Earth where there is an unobstructed line of sight to four or more GPS satellites. Obstacles such as mountains and buildings block the relatively weak GPS signals.
https://www.gps.gov/technical/ps/2008-SPS-performance-standard.pdf
76. Waze – https://www.waze.com/en-GB
77. https://seoexpertbrad.com/voice-search-statistics
78. His Dark Materials by Phillip Pullman (1995)

Microsoft, Cortana; Amazon, Alexa; Google, Assistant[79].
Challenges to consider:

1.  **Compatibility:** Which smart home products and hubs are compatible with which digital assistant? What works with what?

2.  **Updates:** Whether the user can keep up to date with upgraded products and the software operating systems to ensure best functionality and security. What is the upgrade process?

3.  **Safety settings:** How safe is the smart system? Who can access which product? What are the configuration settings for security and privacy and have they been set up correctly?

4.  **Automate or Control?** What does the user chose to automate and what might be better kept under greater control, for example, with unique passcodes rather than blue-tooth/RFID type fobs? How safe are biometric security scanned data to open access points?

5.  **Can you teach your assistant?** How well does the voice training work for whom on which device? What is the flexibility and accuracy with colloquial language and the voice-types of your users? Can your assistant understand you?

Alexa[80], designed and delivered by Amazon, is now integrated with IoT products like Google's Nest thermostat, Philips Hue, GE lamps and Sonos One speakers. As part of a smart home, Alexa can help the user control and dim the lights, lock the doors, adjust the thermostat, and control other smart home devices. As a massive online service and an e-commerce giant,

79. 2017,
https://www.macworld.co.uk/feature/iosapps/siri-vs-google-assistant-3659249
80. Alexa designed by Amazon. Enabling functions include: retrieve audio tracks on Spotify, create to-do lists, online shop, and control IoT (smart home) products. Alexa is delivered through Amazon Echo, a device that acts both as a speaker and a smart-home hub.

Amazon is expanding its market by offering deals specifically through Alexa, and it's been expanding Alexa's functions to include the assistant's capabilities to work with cars[81]. Current reviews highlight Alexa with its smart speaker Amazon Echo Dot[82]. Recently, parents I know received a present of an Amazon Alexa bought especially for their newborn baby. So far, the Amazon Alexa gift box has remained unopened. The newborn baby is fortunate to be in close and intimate contact with its human carers, enabling early bonding attachment, and therefore embarking on its first stages of developing skills in social empathy and language. In 2019, Amazon announced it sold more than 100 million devices[83]. Alexa is useful by playing music and nursery rhymes triggered by voice commands. There might be a danger that human carers might be tempted to over use these tools as a substitute for human contact.

Siri[84] [85], acquired by Apple in 2010, is now delivered by and integrated by Apple into their family of products. Advanced Siri encourages app developers to integrate with Siri. Siri Shortcuts enables the user to customise and program Siri commands, paving the way to apply AI-based voice enabled business communication. In 2018, Apple reported that 500 million users use Siri[86]. My regular scheduled call from a colleague enabled by Siri, during his commute. It works well for us.

81. July 25th 2019,
https://www.cnet.com/news/amazons-prime-day-is-about-to-deliver-for-inves-tors-too
82. https://www.cnet.com/news/best-smart-speakers-amazon-echo-dot-goog-le-home-mini-2019
83. https://www.cnet.com/news/amazon-has-sold-more-than-100-million-alexa-devices
84. Siri, Apple, Main functions: Set alarms, timers and reminders. Get directions. Preview calendar, access music, set up smart home controls, search for knowl-edge. Delivered through Apple products. https://www.apple.com/uk/siri
85. https://www.apple.com/uk/siri
86. https://www.businessinsider.com/apple-says-siri-has-500-million-users-2018-1?r=US&IR=T

Cortana on Skype[87] is being replaced by Alexa and not integrated into its evolving games platform. Many commenters do not believe that Microsoft will be able to overtake this market. Their competitors Apple iOS and Amazon are already ahead of the game, with individual smart home user experience UX at the forefront of their design and development customer approach. GoogleAssistant has the same functions as the others but offers more advanced assistant intelligence[88].

However, any of these digital assistants are being pivoted into the market now through the choice of smart home speaker. Consumers are advised to choose a smart speaker which is smart home system neutral, such as Sonos One. It offers good audio functions that can be used at home whether you use Alexa, Google Assistant or Apple Siri[89]. Apple HomePod has the best audio, but some functionality is limited to Apple products and applications. This works if your home environment is based around the Apple home system.

Which of these will remain in the marketplace does not only depend on their functionality, aesthetic appeal, superior AI, or capability to be secured through customisable configuration settings. The extent of market reach, user distribution, distribution, production and political factors can override the functions and quality of any product in the race to achieve the competitive edge and dominate the market, for example, VHS versus Betamax videotape wars in the late 1970s.

Crucial to production is who controls and has access to the supply of components. The gaining of competitive advantage is determined by the detail of the business partnership deals between the product developers and

87. Cortana – Microsoft , 2019, https://www.cnet.com/news/microsoft-appears-to-dump-cortana-in-skype-for-amazons-alexa
88. https://www.blog.google/products/assistant/google-assistant-going-global
89. https://www.cnet.com/news/best-smart-speakers-amazon-echo-dot-google-home-mini-2019

the corporate component suppliers. Essential computer chip components are supplied by Qualcomm, Taiwan-based MediaTek, China-based Huawei and South Korea-based Samsung. The dominant factor in this competitive race is which computer product supplier, be it Apple, Amazon, Google, Microsoft or another, can access or attain essential component supplies and their intellectual property.

# 1.3

# The ethics of AI. Are humans in control?

People are frightened of AI[90], smart systems and robots, especially if these systems are perceived as autonomous. It seems to the 'reluctantly digital' that the world is changing so fast, the humans are not in control and the system itself is automated and out of control. Let's dive deeper into some smart system examples: Financial Markets; Chatbots; Game development; AI drones in the military; drone wars invading our air space?

## FINANCIAL MARKETS

The bank JP Morgan[91] has created a model to identify the next financial crisis. Data on the length of the economic expansion, the potential duration of the next recession, the degree of leverage, asset-price valuations and the

---

90. AI, artificial intelligence, smart systems. In this context what is relevant is that in these smart systems, feedback and feedforward loops can integrate new data feeds and streams that can reset the system to change and adjust operational pathways and can also be enabled to self-teach/learn new approaches to action commands and could autonomously act on these newly acquired methods and changes to its code.
91. https://fortune.com/2018/09/13/jpmorgan-next-financial-crisis

level of deregulation and financial innovation before the crisis is added to the model. A pattern of peak-to-trough performances are estimated. Their smart system model anticipates the next financial crisis to be in 2020. In 2008, Lehman Brothers bank crashed and initiated a global financial crash. One influencing factor was the US Government push for banks to inappropriately lend to people who could not afford house mortgages. However after analysis it was deemed a systemic failure of complex inter-dependent factors. Can an AI smart system anticipate accurately all the factors, their interdependencies and attributes and the weight of significance attributed to different elements? A smart model will respond to the data, attributes and system functions that are uploaded. But as computer scientists warn – if you put ill-considered data into the system, you will get erroneous conclusions. Scientists refer to this practice as Garbage In Garbage Out (GIGO). We need to carefully consider what we are measuring, how these measurements are being obtained and what interdependent determining factors we need to take into account.

## CHATBOTS

Chatbots offer the user a chance to chat to a side text box, usually in the bottom right hand corner and available within the first moments of logging into a website. The current chatbot application follows conditional logic, giving a response to a query with a pre-formulated response depending what the user enters into the chatbot box. Usually if it does not find recognised search tags it passes the user to a 'human' respondent. This can be slower than navigating to required information within the website. Bots that can negotiate[92] could change this experience by offering a human conversational look and feel. The AI could decide on a path forward on your behalf, enabling developers to create more flexible interactions. Facebook researchers observed how bots were able to generate what seems like a more efficient communication language for bots, but not for humans, in fact bypassing human natural language processing, such as English conceptual numbers, and developing a response more akin to a series of ones and zeros to indicate quantity attributes[93]. What happens if the bots talk to each other in a language humans cannot understand?

## BRAIN SCANNERS

In 2017, Facebook started working on a headband that would let people type at a speed of 100 words per minute, just by thinking. Working with the University of California, San Francisco, researchers have been developing "speech decoders" able to determine what people are trying to say by analysing their brain signals. This early stage research analysed brain signals as people spoke aloud but not their thoughts. If this wearable brain-control device becomes feasible and personal data (including what we are thinking) is downloadable by a giant tech company, neuro-ethicists need to develop an ethical framework and legal regulations on how brain data is collected, stored, and used. The team from UCSF, led by Chang[94] used sheets of electrodes, called

92. https://www.theverge.com/2017/6/14/15799068/chatbot-negotia-tions-ai-facebook-fair
93. https://research.fb.com/publications/word-order-biases-in-deep-agent-emergent-communication
94. Real-time decoding of question-and-answer speech dialogue using human cortical activity; David A. Moses, Matthew K. Leonard, Joseph G. Makin & Edward F. Chang
Nature Communications, volume 10, Article number: 3096 (2019)
https://www.nature.com/articles/s41467-019-10994-4, July 2019.

ECoG arrays, that were placed directly on the brains of volunteers, who were undergoing brain surgery for epilepsy. The aim is a wearable headset that lets users control music or interact in VR using their thoughts.

**GAMING**

Can a user deactivate/destroy AI code functions within virtual game worlds? What does AI mean in this context? In a game development environment this refers to an automated function triggered by sensory input. Sometimes one comes across a plea for help and support from a game developer or player. They cannot re-activate the AI code function, changing their 'pawn' into a 'rag-doll'[95]. Across coding and gaming communities user forums, one can feel their pain[96]. Here is an example of disable AI code on the Unreal Engine developer platform that generates 3D virtual worlds and gaming platforms: _soldier1 **disableAI** "AUTOTARGET". This is just a game, but Serious Games applications[97] develop these straightforward code functions by modelling complexities of real simulations of war and/or rescue strategic operations.

Serious Gaming have developed integrated gaming/VR/AR simulations with integrated smart systems. These are now used in the military, medicine and construction[98] [99] industries to design and prepare, or pre-plan decisions, for real physical world actions. The smart system feeds on data from iteratively generated

---

95. https://forums.unrealengine.com/development-discussion/blueprint-visual-scripting/18429-deactivate-destroy-ai-without-destroying-pawn?46592-Deactivate-destroy-AI-without-destroying-pawn=
96. https://community.bistudio.com/wiki/disableAI
97. https://www.cio.com/article/2371694/pilots--soldiers-and-surgeons-play-serious-games.html
98. https://www.geekwire.com/2016/construction-companies-turn-to-virtual-reality-to-plan-build-and-manage-complicated-projects
99 https://www.ukconstructionmedia.co.uk/news/digital-skills-construction-industry

patterns, probabilities or expectations, but in real life action, at which point will a real human decision-maker need to agree a smart system's decision, for example, when not to shoot/rescue, when to hit or not to hit an auto target? Military and rescue operation teams are developing appropriate systems that enable human override functions and double checked approval systems using semi-autonomous smart systems in order to maximise safety and the protection of human lives. Human override functions need to be coded in.

## AI DRONES IN THE MILITARY

The UK and US military currently use AI drones and in 2019, Marcus Roth[100] explained the range of their functions, from external and indoor navigation, training, reconnaissance and patrol missions. Drones using computer vision technology and image recognition can navigate hostile or unknown landscape without GPS tracking technology. These drones are autonomous, using a combination of emerging technologies including machine vision. Some have the capability to collect data that could allow them to move faster and check if they are being pursued during tactical reconnaissance, tracking, combat assessment and cartographic missions.

Drones are used to explore GPS-denied areas, such as the interior of buildings and caves, to gather mission intelligence; functions can include camera recognition and identification of predetermined targets and then the alerting of a human operator. Capabilities include searching through crowds to find and identify persons of interest. Tasks include inspections of large industrial equipment, like telephone towers, and the capability to generate a real-time damage report.

---

100. https://emerj.com/ai-sector-overviews/ai-drones-and-uavs-in-the-military-current-applications

To counter the threat of drones in illegal air spaces either nuisance or enemy drones, technology has been developed to deactivate drone activities. Qinetiq Global[101] offers products to governments using their Obsidian Counter-UAV system. Here, a combination of 3D radar and camera systems provide robust 3D detection through imagery and video analysis. The DroneShield product range uses radar, camera and thermal multi-sensor analysis to deactivate any flying drone within a range of 2 km[102]. Are these drone wars coming near you anytime soon?

## SMART SYSTEMS IN INDUSTRY

Smart systems are being embedded in most industries. Gaming, VR/AR platforms with related emerging technology including AI and smart systems are now being developed to enhance medical research and practice. Medical AR/VR/gaming applications can facilitate surgical training, for example, Medical Realities[103]. Steve Dann, Chairperson of Medical Realities also chairs the popular seminal Augmented Realities regular monthly Meet Up London, UK[104].

## ETHICS WHEN USING SMART SYSTEMS AND AI

Ethical considerations indicate that any online smart system that includes robotics, autonomous drones and vehicles must be able to be deactivated. Can robots be deactivated? Can we pull the plug before any destructive agencies or the online robotic system gains control? European guidelines have proposed seven key

101. https://www.qinetiq.com/Blogs/2018/08/How-Governments-can-counter-the-threat-of-drones
102. https://www.droneshield.com/how-droneshield-works
103. https://www.medicalrealities.com
104. https://www.meetup.com/Augmenting-Reality/events/262201267

requirements that AI should meet to fulfil the necessary level of trustworthiness[105]. When we design any cyber IT infrastructure it needs to be compliant with regulations that protect against the inappropriate use and potential dangers of AI. In addition, there is a need to be in line with GPDR, which seeks to protect individuals' freedoms and privacy. In summary, European ethics guidelines below, indicate we need to put the 'human agency' and our humanistic ethical values into our systems in order to maintain ethical practices. The EU offers a systematic and robust framework for this crucial cyber challenge. James Elles presents the EU as far ahead in providing a way forward compared to the USA or China[106].

1. *Human agency and oversight:* AI systems should empower human beings so that humans are in-the-loop, humans are on-the-loop, and humans have in-command access.
2. *Technical robustness and safety:* AI systems need to be resilient and secure, with a fall back plan and designed to be accurate, reliable and reproducible.
3. *Privacy and data governance:* quality, integrity, legitimised access.
4. *Transparency:* the data, system and AI business models should be transparent and have traceability. Humans need to be aware of the system's capabilities and limitations.
5. *Diversity, non-discrimination and fairness:* Unfair bias must be avoided, from the marginalisation of vulnerable groups, to the exacerbation of prejudice and discrimination. AI systems should be accessible to all, regardless of any disability,

105. https://ec.europa.eu/digital-single-market/en/news/ethics-guidelines-trust-worthy-ai
106. From a conversation with James Elles, August 2019. Fiction, Fact and Future: An Insight into EU Democracy by James Elles, Haus Publishing.

and involve relevant stakeholders throughout their entire life circle.

6. *Societal and environmental well-being:* AI systems should benefit all human beings, including future generations. They should be sustainable and environmentally friendly. Consideration of societal impact.

7. *Accountability:* Assurance of responsibility and accountability for AI systems and their outcomes. Auditability, which enables the assessment of algorithms, data and design processes. Identification of critical applications.

## NANO-ROBOTS AND AUTOMATION

Nano robots[107] are tiny and hidden robotic particles used in medicine and engineering. They can be radically embedded into our systems and our own biological bodies. In medicine, their use is being developed for drug delivery, anti-bacterial treatments, diagnostic techniques and wound treatments. A stunning photograph of a nano-robot project was 'One hundred tiny painters' by Dr Edmund Hunt, University of Bristol, which received 3rd prize in the Equipment and Facilities category.

> 'In the future, large groups of nanoscale robots could work on tasks such as delivering drugs to tumours. Ants lay pheromones on the ground to communicate indirectly. One behaviour is laying territory-marking pheromone so that other ants know the area has already been explored. Tiny, light-sensitive robots could be manipulated under the microscope in such a way in future nanomedicine.'[108]

107. https://www.understandingnano.com/medicine.html
108. Bristol Robotics Laboratory with Sabine Hauert and Jerry Wright, The Guardian, June 2019.

## WILL AUTOMATION, AI AND ROBOTICS TAKE AWAY JOBS?

Yes, but the workforce will need to re-train to fill the Cyber Technology skills shortage. Whilst a large number of people are being replaced by a smaller number of people using machines, expectations are that courier drivers will retrain as drone pilots, fabric cutters will re-skill as 3D printer managers and car production line fitters will become robot operators[109]. Today people are expected to re-skill a number of times during their career portfolio. We will need to configure and regulate the machines and keep the humans in-the-loop, on-the-loop and reviewing the 'loops' in the systems[110]. Human skills will be appreciated, especially those of system and product design, adaptability, critical and creative thinking, personal one-to-one services, empathy and comprehension; furthermore, skills in the cultural and creative industries and mental health will still be required. Experts in South East Asia pragmatically note in their region, that whilst AI and automation are redefining workplace productivity, efficiency and precision, less employment will be required. If harnessed, AI technologies can contribute to positive social outcomes and machine learning innovations can enhance credit models and enable financial inclusion[111].

109. https://www.raconteur.net/business-innovation/will-automation-create-better-new-jobs
110. https://ec.europa.eu/digital-single-market/en/news/ethics-guidelines-trustworthy-ai
111. https://techcollectivesea.com/2019/05/29/will-automation-take-our-jobs

## CHALLENGING FINANCIAL EXCLUSION

Facebook's recent announcement about its new cryptocurrency[112], Libra, promises to bring financial inclusion to the developing world and isolated areas which lack financial support from traditional banks. Some in the finance world are getting scared at this call, perceiving the aim of global, open, instant[113] movement of money across borders as opening the doors to money laundering, illegal and harmful drug distribution, crime and tax evasion, by producing holdings of a large liquid cryptocurrency without protective barriers to maintain financial stability. How will Facebook's Libra system and network technology mitigate the risk of becoming 'Dark Money' working in tandem with the Dark Net?[114] Facebook reports that Libra is a fast, scalable tool to quickly detect loops, black holes, and other reachability failures in networks with tens of thousands of switches. Libra is much faster than any previous system for verifying forwarding correctness in a large-scale network. They conclude that Libra is just the beginning of bringing distributed computing into the network verification world. This emerging technology now needs to integrate with the checks and balances of the financial world, rather than working outside of its zone.

---

112. Cryptocurrencies use blockchain technology, which is an open distributed ledger that can record transactions between two parties efficiently and in a verifiable and permanent way. Thus the data values are encrypted and not stored in one location but rather distributed online.
113. https://libra.org/en-US/white-paper/#introduction
114. https://research.fb.com/blog/category/systems-and-networking

# 1.4

# Identity, fashion and cultural identity

Cyber fashion, like real world fashion, is a commodity which enables visual statements about who we are, our identity, attributes, affiliations and ethical values. We can be influenced by visual motifs of 'cyber' to make specific design choices. We may purchase online or choose to try and not purchase fashion as a commodity at all. Fashion, like most products today, is created and produced globally, across national boundaries, by means of online communication tools and platforms. In addition, the cyber-self can embody cyber, through wearable computing, or through computer implants within our biological physical bodies. As consumer-citizens, what are we saying about our cyberselves?

**VISUAL CYBER MOTIFS AND CYBER DESIGN METHODS:**

Clothes hide, protect and warm our naked selves, masking our physical differences, whilst fashion seeks to display our identities and values. Identities can be influenced by cultural icons and comic book genres such as Superman, manga and animé. These portray self-obsessed heroes questing for power, sex, tribal identity, romantic love and comradeship. Each character is designed with specific motifs and icons, and dressed to communicate their unique specific qualities.

Clothed and symbolically assigned, the heroic character sets out on the quest. Often in competition, psychologically anguished, the hero's desire is frustrated by enemies or circumstances..

In ancient legacy narratives such as the Epic of Gilgamesh, Psalms, Gita, Iliad, Hiawatha, Beowulf, the story teller tells of a fictionalised coming of age journey, a quest for adventure, power and love. The heroes need to navigate a way forward and negotiate ethical dilemmas. Our sense of a cyberself is built upon this legacy.

Characters and their clothing and props are iconic, through challenges signifying symbolic values. Our online virtual worlds are heavily scaffolded by metaphors and signifiers from a rich hybrid remediated mix of cultural histories. Early career Computer Gaming and Animation designers have presented character and story line research on their favourite influences from their experiences of gaming and media, not aware that these characters and narratives had been based on narratives and characters from the world's ancient histories of myths, legends, folk epics and deep ancient psychological coming of age rituals.

From about 1997, at the start of the digital then online virtual platforms, our avatars/players, and our virtual cyberselves were able to design and build virtual fashion items to dress their avatars. With reference to retro-styles, vintage, DIY style fashion, using inputs from our own camera work, online sourced photos, captured textures, colours, with 'Inworld'[115] and online

115. 'Inworld' refers to the In world experience of avatar or player virtual worlds (gaming). Inside the world of an MMORPG (Massively multiplayer online role-playing game) is a genre of role-playing video games in which a very large number of players interact with one another within a virtual game world.

media tools, we were able to sculpt and design what we will. Today, this capability is enabled through the tools on everyone's smartphone. The designs of physical fashion reflect this use of photo, texture and motif. Simply, the photos we capture ourselves are editable and printable onto t-shirts, mugs and many fashion items. Designers source images from audio waveforms, electrical circuits, motherboards and computer codes reflecting back to us the software embedded in most everyday products.

# 1.5
# Cyber Media

## CYBER MEMES

Integral to cyber fashion and cyber identities, are the cyber memes. Memes are an element of a culture or system of behaviour embodied in a specific image, video, piece of text passed from one individual to another by imitation using an online social platform, often in jest, humour or mimicry, occasionally with cruel spite or satire. In Cybercare, we have identified examples of meme use on SnapChat[116], as a cyber bullying activity where the perpetrators tease the victim by visually editing his/her head onto a football visual object and designing their avatars to kick the football from one to the other – symbolically threatening to 'kick your head in' and thus do the victim harm. Snapchat is a global multimedia messaging application usually used on smartphones. The main feature is to distribute online pictures and messages are usually only available for a short time. Users create, distribute and comment on virtual stickers and augmented reality (AR) objects. AR objects, in this context, are editable mash-up collages, combining real photos with cartoon-style images.

---

116. Snapchat. https://www.snapchat.com/l/en-gb

## CYBER FASHION

Cyber fashion seeks identities that acknowledge the ease of the digital mash-up, or hybridisation. Some of these Cyber fashion identities reflect techno, cutting edge, future shock, a general urban underground vibe. Initially taken up by clubbers within trance and rave music environments, now this vibe is entering mainstream fashion – reflecting android implants embedded within the human form, remediated mix of taboo and electrical circuits, or electronic visualisation of wave-forms. The look and feel of contemporary cyber fashion is generated from a hybridisation of style and identity – as post-apocalyptic, post-industrial, goth, fetish, historical corsets, military. Fashion houses like LipService[117], CyberGoth[118], Cyberdog[119], and CyberFyber[120] pay homage to sub-cultures, micro trends that have emerged through blogs and memes. At Cyberdog, my favourite clothes use a trim with a music equaliser motif.

## CYBERGOTH

Nevena Bjelic[121] identified several micro trends, including Normcore, HealthGoth, GhettoGoth. Normcore is a throwback to retro trends, unisex, what your parents may wear, fitting in with the norm[122]. In comparison, Cybergoth-punk fashion seeks an artificial look and feel, paying homage to rave, industrial, punk and fetish, inspired by sci-fi, and some androgyny. The style can feature one starkly contrasting bright or neon-reactive

117. Lipservice Fashion House https://lip-service.com
118. CyberGothFashion,https://www.iamattitude.com/styles/cybergoth-clothing
119. Cyberdog store and online: https://www.cyberdog.net; Located at Chalk Farm/Camden London.
120. CyberFyber, https://cyberfyber.co.uk
121. Nevena Bjelic, 2016, https://www.rebelsmarket.com/blog/posts/19-of-the-newest-notable-alternative-trends-in-the-last-decade.html
122.https://www.beyondretro.com/blogs/news/the-ultimate-guide-to-normcore-fashion

theme color, such as red, blue, neon green, chrome, or pink set against a basic, black gothic outfit. Matte or glossy black materials such as rubber and shiny black PVC can be mixed and matched in an effort to create a more artificial look. Cybernetic patterns such as live LED circuit boards and electronics, body modification, homage to aviators. Artificial, extended hair or 'falls' can be used to create an added effect made from fluorescent tubing to electrical wiring. Club gear for cyber-goths includes tight black pants, tight black vests or shirts cut from ripped, solid or fishnet fabrics, often resembling costumes from 19th century gothic novels or early black and white horror films from the mid-20th century. Popularised from 2003, today these cyber motifs and fabrics have been assimilated and re-interpreted, influencing street fashion.

## CYBER MOTIFS

Visual motifs based on our emerging cyber experiences can be found on everyday household products. You can get a shower curtain with a visual motif based on electronic circuits[123]. A hybrid of visual motifs are re-purposed from punk, electronics, sci-fi and media. Cyber fashion, DIY fashion, self-created fashion, often utilising the ease of digital photo printing, enables a creative interweave of motifs. These trends show homage to a rich mix of cyber, retro-styles, music clubs and film culture. Image source material all easily accessed via internet and copied, edited, mashed up and printed 2D or 3D using digital media tools and technologies.

---

123.https://www.redbubble.com/people/madjack66/works/39738711-electronic-circuits?p=shower-curtain

# HEALTH AND BEAUTY SOCIAL MEDIA INFLUENCERS

Cyber lifestyle channels include online lifestyle stylists, for example, 'Kat has got the cream'[124], where Kat showcases branded products within her lifestyle narrative, aesthetically presented, creating the look and feel of clarity, precision, artiness of a 'Yummy Mummy'[125]. Business is created via sponsorship deals for product placement. In most cases, these images are a far cry from the reality of real experiences of parenthood and family life. On the other side of the tracks, Jack Munro[126] offers practical hands on skills on 'how to cook for cheap and how not to starve,' using her blog as a single parent trying to feed herself and her child. Several years, books and blogs later, this seems to be paying off with a media team and an online business.[127] Social media influencers who specialise in video logs are known as vloggers[128]. They have generated a proliferation of health and beauty social media. Sofya Aleynikova[129] in her analysis of beauty vloggers, describes a phenomena of paranormal story-times. She interprets these psychological expressions as the acknowledgement of anxieties surrounding social media's increased role in social life. Through the

124. http://www.katgotthecream.com
125. The urban dictionary describes a Yummy Mummy as 'An attractive, healthy, and very sexy mother! Usually a young woman or sometimes a really gorgeous and hot middle aged mother. Yummy mummies usually wear trendy clothes, have great hairstyles and always look fabulous.' This type of phrase is generated from the celeb culture, created from 1980s onwards in a sea of media splashes where celebs would 'work hard' to be the fairy tale princesses living in a fictional palace/castle responding to the perceived needs of a spectating socially aspirational audience.
126. 2012 – https://cookingonabootstrap.com/2012/07/30/hunger-hurts
127. 2019 – https://cookingonabootstrap.com
128. Social media influencers who blog using video are known as vloggers. Vloggers upload a regular online posting of videos, with an online community who follow their blogs.
129. 2019, Sofya Aleynikova, Why Youtubers See Ghosts – Beauty vloggers' paranormal storytimes as neogothic genre Rhizome online community. https://rhizome.org/editorial/2019/jul/05/why-youtubers-see-ghosts

online display of the paranormal stories, a negotiation of internet-induced anxieties about "presence" in the virtual and the material world is evident. These Beauty vloggers are in a sense a community of online artists whose work is an attempt to mediate the tensions about seeing and being seen, feeling and making felt, and the feeling of vulnerability and yet the need to 'show'. As Softa Aleynikova sums up: 'It is a collective exorcism of internet culture demons, a fantastic solution to an equally fantastic problem'.

# 1.6

# Cyber co-creation

The legacy of computer mediated communication tools has enabled cyber co-creation. Today all design is using cyber co-creation, be it 2D graphics[130], media and moving images, fashion, product, landscape or virtual gaming worlds.

The construction industry uses and is developing its use of 3D virtual tools[131]. Enhanced technology capability is being fast tracked in order to develop ways of communicating that can enhance design and production. Communication channels include real time design specifications, coordination and delivery, both within and across teams. They bring together different construction specialists at the same time, same place through VR/AR applications, adding projections of real time timelines and production activities to their wider stakeholders and clients[132]. Creation of virtual world simulations are used as enhanced communication tools to the community by the construction industry. VR solutions enable the

130. Adobe's inter-compatible suite of graphic tools for 2D, 3D and integrated design: https://www.adobe.com/creativecloud.html
131. Autodesk's inter-compatible suite of 3D tools for construction in architecture, building and engineering, 3d Gaming, product design: https://www.autodesk.com
132. https://www.ukconstructionmedia.co.uk/videos/virtual-reality-model-a9-a82-longman-junction-improvement-scheme/

construction industry to communicate design concepts, plans and simulations to stakeholders mainly in the sectors of construction, defence and health.

Cyber technologies can be combined to offer a more complex and intelligent system. XR immersive realities (augmented, virtual or mixed cyber experience) can be combined with smart systems. Smart systems use AI to collect data to feedback into the smart system, to offer new or additional information and insights. The data can be patterns of user engagement or how the user interacts with the XR system.

# 1.7

# From Virtual Community to Meta verse

## SIZE AND INTIMACY OF GROUPS

According to the anthropologist, Robin Dunbar, humans tend to create social groupings of intimate 'family and friends' of about five, then widening out to groups of 15, 50, 150. Based on evolutionary history of community size, this numeric pattern was found to be reflected in social grouping within social media groups[133]. Moreover, these internet friendships, to be sustained, need face to face interaction. Could this be dependent on the limitations of our human brain physiology?

Dunbar found that although there were differences in group size preferences between introverts and extroverts, on the whole, the estimation of relative numbers remained constant. Moreover these relative number groupings were evident online as well as offline. He asked: Why are primates sociable?[134] His research indicated the group size had an impact on

133. https://www.npr.org/2017/01/13/509358157/is-there-a-limit-to-how-many-friends-we-can-have?t=1564780206090
134. https://www.sciencedirect.com/science/article/pii/S0003347207002345

risk from predators: 'Primates that were found to live in groups larger than predicted by their neocortex size usually suffered from greater predation risk'[135]. The larger the group, the less time for intimate contact, and the more likely the risk from predators. Dunbar's findings might suggest that what is important for your best survival, is not the number of social media friends you have, but the quality of the intimacy of communication you might have with your friends. However the size of your optimal group may depend on the physiology of your brain and your personality type.

In our online world, our amount of connections across the internet is expanding exponentially. Could the Internet itself be considered to be a collection of all our brains into one global brain? Could online human-to-human communications reflect an intimate exchange, akin to 'animal grooming', without face-to-face physical interaction?

## GLOBAL SURVIVAL AND TECH FOR GOOD

In the context of the online world, who might be our predators? Social groups and intimate friendships enable greater survival. However, for humans today, our greatest threats are our global and societal challenges.

As indicated, three major global changes include:

1. Socio-economical divisions across populations living in close proximity that have led to political conflict and war.
2. Protection of the environment and the management of ecological change and the careful use of the earth's resources.
3. Cybersecurity of the Information Highway, electronic communication channels and its infrastructure.

135. Lehmann, J., Korstjens, AH., Dunbar, RIM: 2006, Group size, grooming and social cohesion in primates, https://www.psy.ox.ac.uk/publications/288112

Our current need is for both intimate groupings and also memberships of larger influential networks to determine change. As described earlier, some virtual communities and their applications are value-driven and seek to address these global complex and interrelated challenges.

A 'tech for good' application is not just a tool and platform, but a means of establishing a community that will communicate and work together for common goals, values and benefits. Online applications and social media tools can generate effective social grouping, networks and federations of smaller groups. However, within this environment, trust and respect need to be nurtured.

Small groups enable the development of intimacy and trust, face-to-face interaction and some form of kinaesthetic and physical touch. The psychological benefits of small groups, in part, pay homage to the legacy of the 'small is beautiful'[136] movement and is the backbone of therapeutic interventions as evidenced by the pioneering work of the Institute of Group Analysis[137] and others. In our online world, interconnectivity can be fostered between small groups, and federations of communities of common interest can be established, underpinned by processes that enhance trust, respect and related values.

## SOCIAL ONLINE COMMUNITIES

'Medium' is an online community for sharing content by and for writers, thinkers and storytellers focussed on 'fresh thinking and unique perspectives.'[138] The topic features tagged functions which enable the user to

136. E. F. Schumacher. 1973, Small Is Beautiful: A Study of Economics As If People Mattered. The influential concept was that small, appropriate technologies empower people more than 'bigger is better'.
137. The Institute of Group Analysis, 'IGA', https://www.groupanalysis.org
138. https://medium.com

guide their own search pathways, establishing their own special interest groups and sub-communities, providing a customised reading experience and often posting up quite intimate material and exposing personal stories. Why do they feel they can trust enough to feel safe on this platform? How are trust and respect nurtured within this type of platform?

## REGULATION OF SOCIAL MEDIA

Facebook in itself is not the 'evil monster' depicted by some media commenters. 'I think what tends to work well is transparency, which I think is an area where we need to do a lot better and are working on', says Facebook's CEO Mark Zuckerberg[139].

Regulation of these platforms is necessary. In order to regulate and protect, social media channels need to identify and enforce how users use their services. It is necessary to identify codes of practice, methods of watching and monitoring, identification of any harmful communication and to whom. Decisions need to balance the right of individual freedom of speech and thought with the right of individuals to be safe and protected against harm. Decision-making bodies need to be democratic, enabling rather than shutting down debate. They need to establish means of constant revision, responsiveness and listening to the many perspectives across the globe. Are Trump's tweets harmful, ignorant, informative or crucial? Media comments indicate that it is important that worldwide users and populations are exposed to the unmediated thoughts of the President of one of the largest and powerful nation states. How does this exposure influence social and political factors?

139.2018,https://www.wired.com/story/what-would-regulating-facebook-look-like

## UX: UNDERSTANDING USERS AND USER EXPERIENCE

The Internet provides a communal and spatial extension to our physical reality: primarily perceptual and auditory space which can change constantly, both temporally and spatially. Emerging immersive tools open up multi-sensory functions, haptic touch and kinaesthetic choreography. These virtual worlds are accessed by the designing of user control and user interfaces.

## WE ARE VIRTUAL COMMUNITIES, NOT JUST PRODUCTS AND SERVICES

Virtual communities today are essential and pervasive. They exist across local and global communities and then across not-for-profit communities and commercial market sectors. Consider which virtual communities you are in or might participate in. Here are some examples:

Example one:- Scientific communities who wish to share insights and research acumen;

Example two:- Vulnerable and special needs communities who reach out across geographically dispersed areas to other individuals with a common need for services and social interests;

Example three:- Communities of gaming users who compete against contestants across geographical regions;

Example four:- Local councils who seek to involve and engage their communities;

Example five:- Commercial product developers who consult their customers using user forums and consumer platforms to ensure agile development to create competitive and quality products.

Across sectors, the aim is not to directly sell products or services, but to develop communities of users, and understand those users in order to secure and reach new markets.

We are all part of several virtual communities, as a hospital or clinic visitor, a student, a local council resident, a religious, political or special interest organisation. We use online technology directly, by shopping online to receive products through the front door of our home or by purchasing most products today.

Even when we purchase products directly from the traditional high street, from the shop shelf, we are reliant on online business logistic systems. Transportation vehicles are fitted with GPS, VOIP, tracking devices. Logistics and delivery systems function by employing communities of drivers, robot operators, warehouse operatives, all using online systems. These workers form virtual communities networked and dispersed geographically.

We are all participants and users in virtual communities.

## ETHICAL DESIGN OF SOCIAL MEDIA AND IMMERSIVE SPACES

VR designers need to accept the ethical responsibilities of removing a user's entire world and superseding it with a fabricated reality. The unique immersive design challenges for developing VR experiences are intensified when virtual experiences are public and socially-driven. DeRosa and Scherling advocate the importance of acknowledging the language of consent into the design practice of VR in order to design safe, accessible, virtual spaces.[140] [141]

How can virtual worlds and platforms take on the responsibility for monitoring and tracking hate speech and hate crime?[142] Facebook researchers are seeking solutions to automatically track objectionable content such as hate speech, bullying and verbal abuse. Their method integrates, augments and embeds multi-modal media such as text and photo signals to increase identification. Therefore, this type of research can lead to improved enforcement of monitoring social media platforms and the accuracy of reporting to law enforcement agencies.

140.https://research.fb.com/publications/designing-safe-spaces-for-virtual-reality/ accessed 2019.
141. DeRosa, Andrew, and Scherling, Laura, eds, Ethics in Design and Communication, London: Bloomsbury Academic Press, 2020
142. Fan Yang, Xiaochang Peng, Gargi Ghosh, Reshef Shilon, Hao Ma, Eider Moore, Goran Predovic, Exploring Deep Multimodal Fusion of Text and Photo for Hate Speech Classification

# 1.8

# Cyber Art, communities online and virtual worlds

Cyber culture and cyber communities are not only based on IoT, DIY fashion, and work and playing in virtual communities. Cyber art and design activities are having a significant impact on cultural programming, facilitating artists and their audiences; asking questions about who we are as we migrate into our cyberselves. How are we re-formulating ourselves to assimilate and integrate our cyber identities?

How are the museums and galleries supporting the culture of cyberselves? Let's take a dive into some institutions and instances of the Cyber arts and Cyber culture. Let's explore three diverse perspectives: from a major public art organisation, which is internationally renowned – the Tate Galleries, then an online digital artist community – Rhizome[143], and lastly a start-up project PinghubVR with DreamStudio.io[144].

Tate Galleries' curatorial purpose includes the impact of the digital, cyber and computing on art and its audiences. The Tate museums, like all museums

143. https://rhizome.org
144. http://dreamstudio.io; http://www.thepinghub.com/virtual_reality.html

79

and galleries, are changing the way they relate to their audiences[145]. They can use these new technologies to distribute and communicate their services. We live in an increasingly media-saturated world which competes for audiences' attention and engagement. In addition, the new technologies enable artists to engage with and create new creative practices. Museums seek to acquire this digital and online art to curate and interpret it. However, technological operating platforms are evolving and may not be backward compatible with new operating systems. The Tate and other museums and galleries compete in our online world, which offers 24/7 real time culture. We expect instantaneous culture.

net.art is used to describe internet art, often with the internet as its medium but not exclusively, additionally referring to socio-cultural themes of connectivity, global reach, immaterially, interactivity and instantaneity. net.art includes movements that offer satirical responses to internet usage and online social network experimentation. Notably this includes the satirical work of Nam June Paik.

Charlie Gere[146] in his seminal paper with its overview of net.art and its importance, states that this instantaneity is a cause of both euphoria and anxiety. Cyber lifestyle does not insist on boundaries between the home's privacy and all the world outside, confounding inside/outside divisions. The new technologies bring the unheimlich[147] 'other' into the privacy of the home.

Charlie Gere views the traditional ideas of the self

145. Charlie Gere, New Media Art and the Gallery in the Digital Age, Tate papers, ISSN 1753-9854; https://www.tate.org.uk/research/publications/tate-papers/02/new-media-art-and-the-gallery-in-the-digital-age
146. ibid
147. unheimlich – this is not merely unhomely, but refers to Freud's belief that what we find the most eerie or scary originates not from the exotic or foreign, but from what was originally familiar then repressed and subsequently remanifested in an uncanny/unheimlich guise.'

as unified and rooted in one specific culture-bound place, participating in a single national culture, firmly protected from any alien otherness. He sets this idea of the unified self up in opposition to a fragmented divided self. I would argue that this traditional sense of unified self is an illusion. People have always been migrating, whether seasonally or across continents. People's experience is always fragmented, dynamic and emotionally labile. We are not necessarily any more emotionally unstable, anxious or fragmented than in previous epochs. Furthermore, data on trends and change indicates that we have never had it so good[148].

Gere[149] cites Huyssen's proposal that: memory represents the attempt to slow down information processing, to resist the dissolution of time in the synchronicity of the archive, to recover a mode of contemplation outside the universe of simulation, and fast-speed information and cable networks, to claim some anchoring space in a world of puzzling and often threatening heterogeneity, non-synchronicity, and information overload. Huyssen thus suggests the role of the gallery may be a 'place of resistance to' and 'contemplation outside' of the effects of 'accelerating technical processes', through the materiality of the object, in opposition to the fast paced and ethereal digital media. For Gere, the gallery is performative. It creates the past by choosing what to accept as a donation, or to buy, and how to curate, conserve, and display. Today there are many forms of practice it has failed to engage with including: cybernetic art, robotic art, kinetic art, telematic art, computer art and net.art.

---

148. Steven Pinker, 2018, Enlightenment Now: The Case for Reason, Science, Humanism, and Progress

149. [Author's note – an excellent review of the history of net.art, extracted in part. Refer to full paper from Gere] Charlie Gere, New Media Art and the Gallery in the Digital Age, Tate papers, ISSN 1753-9854; https://www.tate.org.uk/research/publications/tate-papers/02/new-media-art and-the-gallery-in-the-digital-age

Gere[150] describes how initial artworks in this area were inspired by the emigration of artists and designers. These artists were connected to Kineticism, the Bauhaus, the Vorticist movement, and displayed at the exhibition 'This is Tomorrow' at the Whitechapel Art Gallery in 1956. In the late 1960s, Buckminster Fuller and Marshall McLuhan offered thinking that gave rise to utopian 'systems aesthetic', in which the combination of new technologies and ideas about systems, interaction and process would produce a better world. Nam June Paik used portable video cameras to produce some of the first video art. The late1970s net-art pointed towards the beginnings of computer special effects, video games, and the beginnings of UX as well as cultural responses such as cyberpunk fiction, techno music and deconstructive graphic design.

Poststructuralism and Postmodernism emerged partly as a critical response to the ubiquity and power of information technologies and communications networks. The writings of Derrida, Baudrillard, Jameson, Deleuze and Guattari and Lyotard proposed a critique that influenced a new awareness around digital and new media works.

In 1997, the Barbican Art Gallery put on the *Serious Games: Art, Technology and Interaction* exhibition curated by Beryl Graham. The emergence of the Web coincided almost exactly with the collapse of the Soviet Union and it was the new-found sense of freedom and the possibilities of cross-border exchange, as well as funding from the European Union and NGOs such as the Soros Foundation that helped foster the beginnings of net art in Eastern Europe, where much of the early work was done.

Gere identifies email listings such as Rhizome, Nettime and CRUMB (Beryl Graham and Sarah Cook's digital curation list based at Sunderland University),

---

150. ibid

seminal work by Lev Manovich, computer art (Nick Lambert)[151] and then a research grant awarded to Birkbeck College, University of London to study net.art.

Despite some moves to feature net.art and the *Matrix: Intersections of Art and Technology* series of talks and the series of talks by well-known curators of new media art held at Tate Modern in Autumn 2003, Gere makes a plea for institutions, the Tate and others to archive and curate net.art and its variations, on the grounds that there are such a large number of artists working in this area. The collection and display of such work will be popular as new technologies affect almost everybody.

The pervasive and ubiquitous nature of emerging technologies are a crucial part of the inter-dependent complex systems that are indicative of the deeper global challenges of our time, i.e. globalisation, genetic manipulation, and bio-terrorism. Whilst these challenges incite audiences' deep anxieties, emerging technologies can also be harnessed towards positive social and global change as indicated by SU[152], WEF[153] and Ray Kurzwell, as noted earlier.

Gere[154] notes that one of the ironies of net.art is that it repeats the gestures of previous avant-gardes. But this repetition of net-art offers a complex relay of anticipated futures and reconstructed pasts. He quotes Foster:

---

151. Nick Lambert, Head of Research, Ravensbourne University [https://www.ravensbourne.ac.uk/staff/dr-nicholas-lambert/] Dr Lambert researches the application of technology in contemporary art and visual culture. He looks at digital and interfaces, and the relation of art and science. He has written on the history of computer art and engaged with artists and theorists in this field. This includes the evolution of interfaces and display technologies. He has developed art works for immersive environments and exhibited in London, New York and elsewhere.
152. SU – Singularity University, USA.
153. WEF – World Economic Forum.
154. Charlie Gere, New Media Art and the Gallery in the Digital Age, Tate papers, ISSN 1753-9854; https://www.tate.org.uk/research/publications/tate-papers/02/new-media-art-and-the-gallery-in-the digital-age

*'The avant-garde work is never historically effective or fully significant in its initial moments. It cannot be because it is traumatic – a hole in the symbolic order of its time that is not prepared for it, that cannot receive it, at least immediately, at least without structural change.'*

We, as the audiences of our contemporary avant-garde, cannot judge the relevance and significance of todays' net.art, for this critique can only be revealed in hindsight.

Rhizome[155] offers the opportunity to present digital artists, commissions, exhibitions, digital preservation, and software development. Founded by artist Mark Tribe as a listserve including some of the first artists to work online, Rhizome identified significant trends within cyber art. Since 2003, Rhizome has been an affiliate in residence at the New Museum in New York City continuing to develop partnerships. This includes The South Bank University[156], which offers a collaborative PhD partnership with Rhizome, NY, examining how best to create user interfaces to access born digital artworks.

In July 2018, PinghubVR and DreamStudio.io, partnering with artists, set out to introduce a variety of extended reality (XR) experiences to the Pinghub network of artists and creatives of artists and creatives, to prepare the way for an immersive platform for use by artists, gallery owners, globally dispersed, to enable greater interconnectivity for their audiences, patrons and artists.

In 2019, Kendal, Mulla and Thomazi[157] investigated

155. https://rhizome.org
156. South Bank University, UK, https://www.lsbu.ac.uk, http://www.lsbu.ac.uk/__data/assets/pdf_file/0005/119273/our-research-environment.pdf
157. Maureen Kendal, Mehmet Mulla, Elaine Freitas Thomazi 2019. How artists can develop their artwork, its market; and deliver their creative content for Virtual Reality environments? EVA conference publication and presentation, 10th July 2019.

how artists from traditional fine art and applied art backgrounds can create innovative immersive and virtual art and build upon their tangible skills, through a digital pipeline and tools. Findings indicated opportunities to co-create partnerships, develop transferable design skills and exhibitions which enable new markets and audiences.

This workshop project identified these considerations:

- Artists' contribution to how it feels to be human and an avatar within virtual world space;
- Concerns around online surveillance and its opportunities for online empowerment;
- Modelling of distribution access to new audiences and re-imaginings;
- A range of viewpoints within this 3D/360 degrees constructed space, affording both close up intimate frames and the wide-long view;
- Artists as digital actors, for example, by placing a 3D model of the artist within their own construction/object/environment or by designing an avatar to resemble an alternative self;
- Artist with headset, as dancing figure, In performative practice;
- Combination of tangible, digital and 'virtual world' production to create new hybrid processes.

For gameplay, the player's agency and the relational schema of interaction needs to be finely balanced to achieve immersion and a reinforced sense of internal mapping and modelling. Balance of a rule-bound world with perceived randomness and user agency is necessary for an interactive immersive environment.

Developing this type of platform there needs to be a consideration of how to implement narrative arcs to enable user engagement. Narrative arcs describe the user journey, often the emotional ups and downs. Often a typical film drama scenario at two thirds into the linear narrative will take the audience into a dip – a place of sadness and defeat, and then this is resolved in the last third resulting in a happy climax at its end. This works well in a linear story. Within an interactive narrative such as in competitive game play within an immersive environment, the narrative arcs of the user's emotional journey are often structured by the user completing one level of difficulty before being allowed to proceed to the next level. So the user's journey is through a series of mini peaks, that offer an adrenaline rush, peaking at the successful end of each level.

User engagement within an immersive platform for artists and creative processes requires a different approach. Creativity is often structured as a series of spiralling activities, in which the artist's creative flow and process may include cycles of deep reflection to re-design, remediate and/or innovate deep structures and elegant design. Creativity often holds in tension – positive creative ideas and an urge to destroy. The artist requires a sense of an internal editor that can hold this tension, reflect, and allow a form of resolution. When building an immersive online platform for artistic and creative activities, interaction with audiences and patrons, the structural design is crucial. Functions may include: studio places to create, exhibition spaces to share, market places to sell, stores of materials and resources, walls for mood-boards and inspirational images. Gallery and platform software like Pinterest, Instagram, Behance[158], and Dribbble[159] often offer these functions.

---

158. Behance is an online platform to showcase and discover creative work. It is owned by Adobe. https://www.behance.net/onboarding/adobe
159. Dribbble is a platform of a community of creative design professionals – on which they can share screenshots of their work, process, and projects. https://dribbble.com

The PinghubVR workshop blends both the physical tangible experience with live immersive shared space and additional live links. Here the pipeline of aesthetic decision-making is a collaboration between artists and specialists. Specialist skills in immersive/interactive arts, composition and experimental music are required to develop VR immersive platforms.

The PinghubVR specialist for music and composition, Dr Elaine Thomazi-Freitas, demonstrated how composing music for the VR immersive environment combines both soundscape and traditional music composition to design the musical thread in VR. The sound space beyond music builds a complex/layered immersive space. The composers – Elaine Thomazi-Freitas[160] and Rosemary Duxbury[161] interviewed traditional artists, and worked with them to translate their memories into music and sounds that were inspired by their cultural and artistic background. Plastic and visual art elements interacted with music and sound to build and define the virtual space as a complex, layered experience.

All participants gained from this opportunity to co-design with these specialist teams using different design languages. Through this pipeline, they were able to integrate their work within their art practice.

The design of interactivity, gameplay, narrative arcs and usability can enrich outcomes of engagement, affordance, market outreach, collaborative benefits, design methods of abstraction, reproduction, and performance.

160. Elaine Thomazi-Freitas, Composer and Sound Artist, Academic – www.thomazi.com
161. Rosemary Duxbury, Composer – www.rosemaryduxbury.com

# 1.9

# Virtual self: Avatar

As we explore the internet, many applications offer us the opportunity to feel at home in the online space by digitally representing ourselves through a pictorial icon, namely an avatar. From basic digital icons to customisable animated and manipulatable characters or players, in online games, and in other non-gaming virtual worlds, these virtual avatars help us anchor, embed and integrate our digital selves into the online environment. Avatars may project a specific personality or persona, or enable a range of functions, skills of an agent or special powers of a non-human angel. Virtual worlds, for example, Second Life (SL), can offer a choice of customisable avatars, ways to create a digital fashion wardrobe with capability to import jpeg files to create unique textures and fabrics; ways to represent your avatar with unique combinations of settings – by altering hips, lips, height, shape, many aspects of physique such as hair, lips, skin colour. Virtual communities ask the user to upload a real life photo or pixelated version or chose an anime style cartoon.

## AVATAR AS CHARACTER, PLAYER OR ROBOT

A human user might create many different avatars, like a writer of a novel imaginatively conjuring up a range of diverse characters. The avatars are controlled by a user account which in reality might be controlled by users other than the user of the original account. Identities of avatars can be interchangeable. Online you may not be talking to who you might think the avatar is representing. Moreover, avatars are not always controlled by a real user, but can be programmed to act as if a real user or represent a role – such as a pre-programmed guide, a non-player character or a ChatBot. For some, their avatar might be an incarnation of their fantasies and dreams. For others, it might seem to be unprotected space, open for the projection of selves that have no rightful place within a real world informed by ethics and empathy. The online world requires a regulatory framework and law enforcement that can balance human rights of free speech and privacy with safeguarding safety, upholding ethics and the common good.

## LIVING IN VIRTUAL WORLDS

In the 1990s, education experts feared that the illiterate would be excluded from the benefits of the 'information super highway'. However, today the data suggests that the benefits of the internet in terms of education outweigh the exclusion of the illiterate. Text is now superseded by moving images and sound. Babies have access to screens and learn how to control interfaces with finger gestures to access media rewards such as children's songs and cartoons[162].

The most widely used virtual avatar creative world from early-2000s is Second Life, SL, created by Linden Labs. Philip Rosedale is the CEO of Linden Labs (LL). He had dreamt about virtual worlds since his childhood and in 1994 he first thought of connecting computers

162. http://besser.tsoa.nyu.edu/impact/s94/students/Jaye/Jaye_asis.html

via the Internet and creating a virtual world. In 1999, he founded Linden Labs, LL, which created and now runs SL. By 2013, SL had approximately one million regular users; at the end of 2017 active user count totals 'between 800,000 and 900,000'.

Second Life, SL, is a large 3D virtual world accessible via the Internet. The content is managed and created by SL users called residents. Residents can communicate, build environments, give presentations, simulate real or imaginary systems, theatre productions, fashion shows and performance, and trade using virtual trade and a type of cryptocurrency, the Linden Dollar. SL is similar to massively multiplayer online role-playing games; however, SL is not a game: 'There is no manufactured conflict, no set objective'. The avatar-resident-users create the rules, the parameters, the landscape, the object, their characters, how and what they create. Sometimes they simulate real shops and cities – there is a Virtual London. Others create bespoke versions of museums and art galleries or fashion outlet or product design.

SL has been used for education and training and is full of creative, imaginative and intelligent people who have become residents and present themselves as virtual avatars. Alan Hudson and the author Maureen Kendal ran a virtual university during 2005–2012, as part of a curriculum for courses in London Metropolitan University. SL was used by several facilities including media, social science, computing and science. In 2011, Alan Hudson and the author created a handbook for using 3D virtual platforms like Second Life[163]. Alan created simulations to teach computer coding, scientific processes and health and safety training. Our SL university worked with

163. Maureen Kendal and Alan Hudson, 2011, On the Beach – A handbook for using 3D virtual digital platforms like Second Life – 'the WEISL' – 'Writing Explorations in Second Life', Electronic Visualisation and the Arts (EVA, BCS conference paper, 2011), https://ewic.bcs.org/content/ConWebDoc/40570

students and staff to design specific areas to address the needs of the curriculum and interests. The region of four islands offered traditional classrooms and lecture spaces, to include specialist interests, for example, a scientific meeting area with simulations of specialist research, a social scientist specialist area, a disco ballroom, a football stadium, a mosque, an open beach with deck chairs, a garden and orchard with mediation levitation cushions. Our curriculum included lessons in communication, research, writing, teamwork, product design, problem-solving, product management, SL travel with geographical orientation and geo-marking, translation tools, moving image and video and communication tools. Exploring 3D digital design included landscape design, the use of immersive 'physics' and 'qualities of attributes such as gravity, flexibility, fabric tension', fashion shows and performance, textile design and historical costume. Additional SL summer workshops were run for prospective college students to explore the opportunities afforded by digital 3D design, gaming, animation and visual effects, from which they were able to design and build their own 'ideal' universities.

Ethical and socially accepted behaviour in the SL world, in some of its islands and regions, has been in the past, the subject of media speculation. A few SL residents were using SL regions to practice unorthodox sexual practices, for example, involving avatars dressing up as furry creatures and taking part in orgy type activities. Having worked extensively in SL for a number of years and explored many regions across the SL world, I only once came across this type of activity in another region. In general, SL was used by educational services and universities to simulate environments and experiences for training and research or by users who created fashion, media or 3D production of content for virtual trade.

SL does not feature the same firewalls and restricted access that can safeguard and protect online public or private systems, such as in a school, public library, or corporate organisation. The SL experience is similar to walking in a public street where you, as an avatar, can see and interact with other avatars. Whilst some unfettered human behaviour can be reflected by a small minority in SL, the owner of any island or region can ensure invisibility, security, restricted access and impose ethical or acceptable behaviour codes on their residents. When we ran our SL university, we left our 'islands' open to visitors, but we agreed on ethical standards, appropriate behaviour and a system to monitor and enforce this across our region. We observed some other islands used restrictive access functions to protect their avatar residents, for example, a girls' college in a religiously observant country and we understood that some national organisations had SL islands that were completely invisible and hidden to any other avatars and regions. Throughout its development, changes to SL's Terms of Service have aimed at bringing user activity into compliance with various international laws, even though the person running the business may be in full compliance with the law in their own country. As a virtual world that is open to its users with global access, SL have faced and dealt with challenges in terms of fraud, banking, socially inappropriate behaviour and illegal activities, for example, online gambling.

Educational and healthcare outcomes are evidenced by research in SL[164]. The relationship of avatars or virtual personas to the 'real' or actual person indicate that virtual selves shape users' offline attitudes and behaviour. Virtual lives and physical lives are not independent of each other. Our appearances and

164. https://en.wikipedia.org/wiki/Second_Life

actions have both online and offline consequences. Real individuals can choose to create multiple avatar selves. It was found that SL residents enacted multiple avatar-self relationships and cycled through them in quick succession and that these avatar-self relationships might be shaped and activated strategically in order to achieve educational, commercial, or therapeutic outcomes. On our SL virtual university, we used different avatars to represent our 'lecturer' role, 'personal' role, 'specialist designer' or 'police-monitor' roles.

## SEEPAGE FROM THE VIRTUAL TO THE REAL

Working in SL to develop and deliver a virtual university, it was common to observe seepage from the virtual experience to the real world (Hudson and Kendal 2007–2011)[165] SL offers a 3D interactive world, with wardrobes of objects that are collectable, modifiable, exchangeable. Avatars can build, fly, walk, dance, chat, and interact in many 'real' ways. Real students in the physical real world would start dressing like the virtual avatars and their wardrobes of clothes that they had been designing 'Inworld'.

After engaging in structured virtual experiences at the Virtual University, they would come into the real classroom with ideas and objects that reflected their personal unique virtual classroom experiences.

'InWorld', their 'virtual classroom' had been located on beaches with deck chairs to sit on, apple tree orchards, helicopters, flying carpets and sunken ships to explore and travel with. Tasks included research, team-working, writing, designing 3D objects, coding, creating digital 'theatre' and fashion shows for an avatar live audience.

165. In conversations between Alan Hudson and Maureen Kendal 2005 – 2012

For Guest[166], the virtual economy intensifies the seepage between the real and the virtual. Virtual cash can be bought with real cash. People can use their avatar selves to design (or 'script') objects and animations and then sell them through SL shopping market. These can include: sunglasses, hairstyles, animated objects, actions and positions for their avatar. Anshe Chung (real name Ailin Graef), an avatar dealer in SL, became the first person to achieve a virtual value worth a real $1m.

Within London Metropolitan University's SL Virtual University, students would work on individual design tasks separately but in the same area. As they worked, they would be discretely watching others at work. It was observed that their design work was influenced by each other. This 'parallel play' was similar to children in the playground semi-consciously mimicking each other. Often the tutors would find students in the virtual university 'On the Beach' classroom at all hours of day and night, immersed in their design tasks, learning from others - whether overtly through chat or covertly through observation and investigating the virtual environment. The 'On the Beach' environment offered a sense of calm and freedom to imagine.

166. Guest, T. 2007, Second Lives: A Journey Through Virtual Worlds, Hutchinson.

# 1.10
# Who is protecting us?

Developing virtual and cyber worlds has taught us that all spaces, be they virtual or physical, need protection, security, privacy and ethical standards. Unfortunately, we cannot live in the Garden of Eden. Within the cyber world, we, like the mythical Adam and Eve, are exposed to a tree of knowledge; this time it is a forest of interconnected networks of knowledge and information. This information superhighway is globally connected, including a large range of different cultures and diverse social expectations. We need to regulate our online worlds as well as being able to engage in creative exploration, innovation and experimentation. Moreover, we need to provide regulatory checks and balances to ensure personal freedom and that minorities are not tyrannised and oppressed.

Countries in the developing world and developed world are seeking to identify best practice and regulatory frameworks to best protect their citizens. There are competing business and political interests. Will the encouragement of creative partnerships offer a balance between the needs of communities, small and medium sized enterprises (SMEs) and the dominating interests of large business organisations?

Who will accept the responsibility of protecting the citizen? From a capitalistic perspective, citizens are free to protect themselves and use their acquired or inherited economic means to do so. From a state socialist perspective, citizens may be monitored for their own protection and state security by a Nanny state. However, in the UK or in other mixed economies, there is an attempt to achieve a balance between state protection and individual freedoms.

The UK Government seeks to provide cyber essential and cyber safe advice for individuals, small businesses and large organisations. Various legal regulations such as Data Protection laws (GDPR)[167] support and protect individuals' privacy, and seek to regulate organisations with dominating economic power to abide by these laws in order to protect the privacy and security of individuals, their communities and organisations.

Social media networks and online business platforms seek to acquire customer relationship marketing (CRM) data for each individual or organisation, in order to provide customised and personalised advertising and promotions to specific target markets. For example, people around retirement age may get targeted by cruise holidays, genealogy businesses, or private health services or insurance plans. Customers might buy online a specific product, and then will be offered similar or related products next time they use that online shopping platform. The online platform and its CRM smart system has identified your tastes and preferences and now is able to 'anticipate' your new requirements. The more you shop and make decisions on that platform, the more 'clever' the smart system seems to become and more accurately 'anticipates'

---

167. GDPR – European Legal Framework for Data Protection.
https://www.gov.uk/government/publications/guide-to-the-general-data-protection-regulation
https://gdpr-info.eu

your next potential shopping decisions. And yet luckily we are human, and thankfully we are fickle, and often what the system 'anticipates' for you, just may not be what you are looking for. The next generation of smart systems are already identifying what type of shopper you are: an early adopter gravitates towards new IT gadgets; a reluctant digital engager avoids new IT products; someone who is curious and buys 'out of the box' products or social experiences; someone who has identifiable habits always goes to specific cultural or social events or someone who always looks for bargains and special offers. Moreover, the system can identify that you only buy luxury items, due to a specific trigger, for example, at a particular time of the week or month and will choose to target you when that trigger or alert is activated. As systems get smarter and are capable of dealing with complex decision-making by its users, we will get more and more dependent on the systems, as they 'help' us to make consumer and citizen decisions. These smart systems can enhance our cyber lifestyles, enabling us to create more sophisticated fashion identities, to design aesthetic and energy-efficient homes and gardens, to widen our choice of food preparation, to identify appropriate life partners and friendship or interest groups, to obtain better healthcare and education. Thankfully, humans are curious, fickle, creative and naturally rebellious so smart systems should enable multiple choices, design decisions and opportunities rather than a closing down or reduction of choice.

Social media networks are capable of tagging and monitoring specific words, phrases or images uploaded by individuals. These smart system processes can identify individuals' political affiliations, social and cultural interests, and purchasing choices.

Large companies, be they social media giants, or online

product distributors, or IT network infrastructures, seek to understand their customers in order to maintain or develop their market reach. An in-depth understanding of the needs of each individual consumer enables smart intelligence and complex CRM that identifies clusters and types of consumer and individual lifestyles.

How do the large companies develop this business understanding about their consumer and users, and how do they build their relationship with their consumer communities? In addition, they need to build evidence on the effect of corporate social responsibility programmes in order to present themselves as ethically attractive to the customer.

There are ways of bringing people and different interest groups together to provide outcomes of mutual benefit. These methods may include creative partnerships, corporate social responsibility (CSR) programmes, sponsorships from large companies in tandem with government programmes. Stakeholders become partners. This can include – the individual, SME, and their communities, corporate sponsors and government. Here government can provide mutually beneficial directives, codes of practice and supportive regulation.

As enhanced online individuals, we can utilise the power of social media collective action, work with CSR, corporate sponsorship and government programmes, in order to  actively design our cyber lifestyle, and shape our identity and power as cyber citizens and cyber consumers.

# 1.11

# Branding and value added support services

Oliver Littlewood (2019) reported that whilst the smartphone industry has become increasingly saturated and the brands fight for market share, retaining customers that are loyal to a brand is a major strategy for manufacturers. Loyal customers ensure long term profitability[168]. Even if you as a customer are dissatisfied with a product, or its support service, will you change brands? This small sample survey found that brand loyalty has a significant impact on price inelasticity and preference to maintain a long term relationship with the brand, despite some product dissatisfaction. Many of us will pay higher prices to buy Apple products or well-known Android brands like Samsung.

However, a deeper dive into an individual user's requirements and purchasing behaviour might look into the more complete user experience to include how easy the phones are to configure, to switch off tracking, to configure privacy settings, to add devices into a comprehensive IT system (clouds, laptops and smart

168. O. Littlewood, 2019, The Effect of Brand Loyalty on post purchase satisfaction amongst Generation Z customers within the UK smart phone industry, Dissertation – Sussex University

homes IoT devices) and to troubleshoot challenges. Some brands offer high street shop support, for example, Apple Stores or PC World or from within mobile phone stores. Are purchasing choices influenced by face-to-face support availability in urban high density areas? Cybercare clients use both non-Apple and Apple brands. In the UK, Apple smartphones dominate the market share even although they seem to cost more. The Apple devices offered integrated software, media applications and greater usability and support choices. A crucial factor that maintains this dominance is maybe the availability of local Apple Stores in urban shopping centres with bookable face to face support with Apple devices. In 2019, in direct competition with Apple Stores, Microsoft[169] have recently opened a high street store with support services for Android phones, Microsoft software, and in-store workshops to promote gaming and VR demos, in Regent Street, Central London, UK.

Traditionally, Apple laptops have been designed for the top end consumer market, whilst other PCs and laptops were designed for office and business use which presumed an office IT support team, and a customised configuration for that specific business environment. Smartphone Android developers wishing to capture the dominance of Apple devices may compete on cost and function but can they offer the resources of the Apple community of users online and face-to-face support? This includes free education, training within shops and online as well as highly resourced security and privacy trouble-shooting system.

169. https://www.microsoft.com/en-gb/store/locations/england/london/oxford-circus/store-1144

# 1.12

# Reaching out to diverse communities

Cybercare[170] offers cyber awareness workshops and support to community groups including the vulnerable, disabled and elderly. Clusters of individuals are using old second hand phones and devices, often unable to update the operating system's updates or application updates. This places the most vulnerable groups in our society at the greatest risk of cyber intrusion and hacking. Users with communication difficulties, or with physical disabilities maybe digitally reluctant and have unexpected challenges.

There is a sharp decline of physical disabilities due to improved obstetric care and foetal defect screening programmes. So programmes for the disabled may need to combine a greater range of disability within the same numbers of people in order to create a sizeable group. Online platforms are therefore customising their applications, features and functions for greater diversity of disability.

There are challenges for people with disability to keep up with commercial expectations, as consumers with special needs or disabilities can be perceived to

---

170. Cybercare, 2019, cybercare.org.uk

be soft consumer targets for assertive sales people. Moreover, very soft targets are non-English speaking consumers with disabilities. There is an invisibility of special and disability needs and a lack of specialist awareness training for many technology sales people. Our witness, Daniel, reports from a deaf perspective that Chatbots are useful, but they are very small and may use lots of text to explain the problem; some consumers use sign language, for example, British Sign Language (BSL) and cannot always have the right vocabulary in English to use Chatbots effectively[171].

---

171. Testimony from Daniel, hard of hearing personal experience and advocate, June 2019

# PART 2:

# ETHICS FOR THE DIGITAL WORLD

## DIGITAL TRUST AND PRIVACY

Trust is the cornerstone for any economy, especially the digital economy (Dobrygowski and Hoffman, 2019)[172]. Corporate companies recognise the economic benefits of putting safety and protection online procedures in place. Being competitive goes hand in hand with investing in 'digital trust'. A mechanical reliable and technical system needs to deliver a trusted service. This needs to go hand in hand with relational trust, whereby rules, codes of practice and shared agreements on how, when, where, why to use which technologies are agreed. The combination of these technical tools and legal rules offers a framework to ensure trust. This framework needs to evaluate accountability, ability to be audited, transparency, ethics, and equity within online business relationships and exchange of goods. Who is accountable for breaches in cybersecurity?

172. Daniel Dobrygowski, William Hoffman, 28th May 2019, We need to build up 'digital trust' in tech, Wired Opinion, Online.

When a breach is evidenced, can it be established who committed the breach?

In May 2019, San Francisco's board of supervisors banned the use of facial recognition software. This was the first major American city to block a tool that many police forces use to search for criminals. The fear is that the US will become an overly oppressive surveillance state like China. The concern is that facial recognition software is incompatible with a healthy democracy. However, even smartphone users can use facial recognition to unlock their devices, and to tag and sort photos.

## POWER AND CONTROL

There is a paranoid perception that data analytics, in the service of CRM and capitalist commodification, is a pervasive and damaging disease. Our work in Cybercare sometimes finds us working with elderly and vulnerable clients who observe 'normal' marketing and sales techniques but perceive these as the system or government  out to get them. Speakers on the media channels often voice an opinion that warns against the dangers of social media companies and data analytics. There is a general fear and lack of education about how to spot a scam, and how to avoid targeted marketing techniques. Social media companies are themselves being targeted as bastions of capitalist commodification by leftist politicians and then as competitive disrupters by rightist politicians and nation states. Which is fact? Both in a sense are true – emerging technology can offer customised and personalised services to consumers using tracking of consumer online behaviour; in addition, emerging technologies are putting traditional businesses such as high street fashion retail shops out of business. In order to mitigate the effects of the fast changing technology landscape, there is a need for global, national legal regulation, with checks and balances to guard against untruthful advertising, infringement of human rights and the abuse of business or state monopolies. Social media in itself is not the big threat but the threat comes from the way social media is regulated and the way people use social media applications. Social media consumers need to be educated in how to use the technology and of the dangers of open networks, of opening accounts using open networks, and the basics of cybersecurity. We would not let untrained children on to a dangerous, busy road without teaching Highway Code fundamentals and the necessity of crossing using traffic lights and traffic interchanges with pedestrian walkways.

China's social credit system[173] is a tool of mass surveillance, using big data and AI-enabled processes to award all citizens a social credit score based on their social, political and economic behaviour. Sci-fi scenarios like Orwell's novel *1984* or episodes of *Black Mirror* feature this type of dystopian society. People with low scores are banned or blacklisted from accessing services including flights and train travel; while those with high scores access privileges. The Chinese Government aims to have all of its citizens subject to the system by 2020.

Furthermore in China, facial recognition is used to monitor the Urghurs, a Muslim minority. The government is already deploying facial recognition technology in Xinjiang, a Muslim-majority region in western China where tensions between ethnic groups erupted in deadly riots in 2009. Reporters from *The Wall Street Journal* who visited the region found surveillance cameras installed every hundred meters or so in several cities, and they noted facial recognition checkpoints at

173.https://www.theguardian.com/world/2018/jun/28/chinas-social-credit-system-could-interfere-in-other-nations-sovereignty

gas stations, shopping centres, mosque entrances, and elsewhere. 'This is the kind of thing that makes people in the West have nightmares about AI and society,' says Subbarao Kambhampati, president of the Association for the Advancement of Artificial Intelligence (AAAI) in Palo Alto and a computer scientist at Arizona State University in Tempe[174].

174. https://www.sciencemag.org/news/2018/02/china-s-massive-investment-artificial-intelligence-has-insidious-downside

# 2.1

# Protecting our online identity

In line with the UK Government's directives, Cybercare UK works with individuals to support them with their cyber lifestyle and understanding on how to use privacy and security settings across a wide range of products and platforms.

**FRAUD AND SCAMS**

Action Fraud enables citizens to report cyber fraud, and to establish their own local area neighbourhood watch schemes, offering opportunities for people to get involved and help themselves and their neighbours combat crime and anti-social behaviour. Neighbourhood watch schemes could set up opportunities, for example, tea-time get togethers to use the National Cyber Security Centre (NCSC) toolkits[175] to support each other against cyber fraud. In the UK, the NCSC[176] and Get Safe Online/Cyber Aware programme[177] [178] promotes the Take Five[179] [180] message:

175. https://takefive-stopfraud.org.uk/take-five-tea
176. https://www.ncsc.gov.uk
177. https://www.ncsc.gov.uk/section/information-for/individuals-families
178. https://www.getsafeonline.org
179. https://takefive-stopfraud.org.uk
180. https://takefive-stopfraud.org.uk/advice

1. Requests to move money – Don't;
2. Click on links – Don't;
3. Personal information – Don't give;
4. Don't assume an email or phone call is authentic;
5. Don't be rushed or pressured into making a decision.

Take Five provides toolkits for families and for organisations to mitigate risk from scammers and Cyber Fraud[181]. There is a rise in Cyber Fraud as the biggest world cybercrime trend of 2019, with advanced phishing and remote access attacks. Sixty per cent of cybercrime is happening through smartphones. Vulnerabilities in home automation and the Internet of Things (IoT) are the next soft targets. As all business, criminal activities are gearing up to maximise access and profit by using smart systems with AI to enhance their phishing and social engineering activities[182].

## MAKING YOUR INTERNET ENABLED HOME PRODUCTS SECURE (IOT)

The UK Government has designed and developed a Code of Practice for Consumer IoT Security[183] for manufacturers, with guidance for consumers on smart devices at home. In practice, there are challenges with different products using different broadband grids, and different ways to guide users to use their products.

Everyday products and internet enabled devices in our homes are often connected to the internet; they are becoming part of the IoT and can make people's lives easier and more enjoyable. When you, as a consumer,

181. https://takefive-stopfraud.org.uk/take-five-tea
182.https://www.weforum.org/agenda/2019/03/here-are-the-biggest-cybercrime-trends-of-2019
183.https://www.gov.uk/government/publications/code-of-practice-for-consumer-iot-security

link up to the Internet, you register your personal data to online devices and services. The cybersecurity of these products is now as important as the physical security of our homes. The aim of this Code of Practice is to support all parties involved in the development, manufacturing and retail of consumer IoT with a set of guidelines to ensure that products are secure by design and to make it easier for people to stay secure in a digital world. The Code of Practice promotes good practice in IoT security. It has been developed by the Department for Digital, Culture, Media and Sport (DCMS), in conjunction with the NCSC, and follows engagement with industry, consumer associations and academia. The Code was first published in draft in March 2018 as part of the Secure by Design report[184]. David Rogers, the CEO of Copper Horse, UK[185], is the author of this code of practice, and was awarded an MBE in recognition of his services to cybersecurity in The Queen's Birthday Honours List 2019[186].

User experience methods and measures, also known as UX or traditionally as Usability Heuristics, indicate that best design practice is to ensure that the user will only need two or maybe three clicks to be able to access, change and activate privacy and security settings on any device. This is to ensure ease of use. In the products and devices using IoT around homes and communities – following some testing by Cybercare – this is often not the case. At the time of testing, Apple products conformed to UX; some Android applications and smart meter device settings were often too deep, needing more than two or three clicks to set up and did not conform to UX best practice.

184. https://www.gov.uk/government/collections/secure-by-design
185. https://www.copperhorse.co.uk
186. https://www.copperhorse.co.uk/tag/david-rogers

# 2.2

# Cyber abuse by whom, why and where

Cyber technology can enable human rights, freedom of information and who controls the communication networks, channels and platforms, and who controls the pervading ideology. If not appropriately regulated and secured, access to cyber communications can facilitate cyber abuse by criminals seeking to financially defraud their victims, by people who lack mental stability such as terrorists and malevolent nation states.

Ideologies are the system of ideas that underpin how we understand our world. Different cultures and nation states promote diverse ideologies. Many, but not all, aim to promote ethical values of truth, justice, compassion and globally agreed principles of human rights. These values underpin delicate balances and checks within our legal regulatory framework.

On social media channels and within popularised culture, we are bombarded by political messages, media stories, statistics and data. We might well consider who says what to whom and why. What do they stand to gain by their message? What do we understand by what is said? Do we believe or trust who speaks and what they say? Is it true or 'fake news'? How is freedom of speech enabled or restricted within the cyber world, where technically we can speak to everyone, 24/7, pervasively, globally? Speech can be powerful, it can create revolutions, uprisings, it can 'let my people go' or promote enslavement.

In response to the aftermath of the Arab Spring, in 2012, Ramesh Srinivasan reported from Egypt[187]:

> "We may forever debate the importance of social media in the uprisings of 2011 in the Arab world's most populous nation. Some argue that social media empowered activists to coordinate and communicate the actions that sparked the revolt. Others, in contrast, argue that social media was a double-edged sword, and in some cases prevented activists from directly confronting the old regime. Skeptics point out that regimes are effective at using technologies to spy and subvert, citing Iran's Green Revolution of 2009. Further, they argue that less than 5% of Egyptians use Facebook and/or Twitter."

One year later in 2013, he reported that the use of online networks was overpowering the state. He reports:

> "Instead of staying within the walled gardens of Twitter or filter bubbles of Facebook, activists have now turned to a new powerful strategy: bridging offline and online. The online world has always supported communication between activists and youth of different

187.Ramesh Srinivasan 2012, https://www.aljazeera.com/indepth/opinion/profile/ramesh-srinivasan.html

stripes and today features increased hacking, leaking and misinformation between political adversaries."

He describes how online social media strategies worked together with an offline strategy of copying, signing, and distributing. Other campaigns used videos simply projected in physical public spaces, re-distributing political content that was once online. The offline strategy follows and is in line with the online distribution to the digital class. Political messages in the form of videos in public places are spreading rapidly and without any formal control to a non-digital population that is dominantly offline[188].

As citizens, we fear the unknown, and we are quickly moving into a new era where our lives are interconnected by the internet. We perceive a lack of regulation but we cannot put our heads in the sand or take on a Luddite[189] mindset. Government and law enforcement agencies working with the cybersecurity industries have identified clusters of cyber-criminals by using computer triangulation and tracking methods. This organised cybercriminal mafia are globally distributed and operating under different legal jurisdictions. Using multi systematic approaches, cybercrime is being systematically rooted out. As cyber citizens we also need to take responsibility, to report cyber abuse and cybercrime, and to take on sensible measures to protect ourselves.

As cyber-citizens, we may work with the police to combat online crime; this might involve reporting online crime to Action Fraud, to your local police

188. Ramesh Srinivasan 2013,
https://www.aljazeera.com/indepth/opinion/2013/07/201374143947684159.html
189. https://en.wikipedia.org/wiki/Luddite: 'one opposed to industrialisation, automation, computerisation, or new technologies in general.'

station, or by using online forms[190]. However, if no one is in immediate danger, the reporting of crime or anti-social behaviour is currently not facilitated by their online reporting system. Action Fraud asks victims of fraud and scams to report to them, when they might offer first response support, obtain information and investigate patterns of online criminal activity.

Policing often involves dealing with people with repeating mental health and addictive issues, preventive activity, and more recently abuse within online communities and /or personal relationships. Domestic crime that includes repeated targeted abusive behaviour can be found in relationships or situations where there is a trio of unhealthy activities such as addiction, mental health and abuse. Cyber abuse can be part of the pattern of physical and or financial abuse and emotional coercion. This type of domestic or neighbourhood crime is usually referred to community safety units within the local police force. Whilst domestic crime does not have the media interest in comparison to terrorism, fraud or 'more sensationalist' forms of murder, two women are killed each week by a current or former partner in England and Wales according to the UK Office for National Statistics (2016)[191]. In the majority of cases, stalking and/or online stalking is evident prior to these homicides. In 2018, Cressida Dick[192] reported that[193] 'the Met receives an emergency call related to domestic abuse every 30 seconds and handles 47 new allegations of rape or other serious sexual offences every day, while recent years have also seen drastic

190. https://www.met.police.uk/ro/report/asb/asb/report-antisocial-behaviour/report-someone-behaving-in-a-way-that-concerns-me
191.https://www.refuge.org.uk/our-work/forms-of-violence-and-abuse/domestic-violence/domestic-violence-the-facts
192. Cressida Dick was appointed Commissioner of the Metropolitan Police Service (MPS) in London in 2017.
193.https://www.stylist.co.uk/visible-women/cressida-dick-met-police-domestic-violence-women-girls/193111

increases in reports of sexual and physical child abuse, child sexual exploitation and grooming.' She attributed these rises in reporting to 'a growing confidence to come forward', but acknowledged that police were currently only 'dealing with the tip of the iceberg', particularly in regard to 'isolated communities'. The nature of these crimes, which often take place behind closed doors, means that they can be extremely difficult for the police to 'uncover, investigate and prosecute'. At our Cybercare desk at a One Stop Shop for Domestic Abuse, it is estimated that over 1 in 4 clients who report domestic abuse, also include extensive cyber abuse. Cyber abuse, in this context, is difficult to evidence for prosecution. Cybercare offers support and advice to victims and survivors of cyber abuse, on how they can protect themselves and their online lifestyle.

# 2.3

# Personal eSafety: Protecting our children and families

The UK Government offers advice on helping your child have safe and enjoyable experiences online[194]. As cyber citizens, as parents, and as members of family groups and communities, we have a responsibility to protect our children and other groups of vulnerable people. 'Personal information gathered online can be misused and result in things like spam, scams, fraud, unwanted contact and grooming or even identity theft.'

> "Unwanted contact is any type of online communication that your child finds unpleasant or confronting, or that leads them into a situation where they might do something they regret. This can happen even if they initially welcomed the contact. It can come from strangers, online 'friends' your child has not met face-to-face, or from someone they actually know. At worst, it can involve 'grooming' a child — building a relationship with a child in order to sexually

194. https://www.esafety.gov.au/parents/skills-advice/privacy-child

abuse them. This abuse can happen in a physical meeting, but it increasingly occurs online when young people are tricked or persuaded into sexual activity on webcams or into sending sexual images"[195].

More sophisticated identify theft can occur by using 2D photographic images or 3D model prints of people's faces and heads, and then these can be superimposed onto video and images of human bodies and used for illegal purposes such as porn, accessing bio-metric security access points or other illegal activities.

195. https://www.esafety.gov.au/parents/big-issues/unwanted-contact

# 2.4

# Cyber-Addictive tendencies and Cyber-Health

The use of computers, social media and computer games can be addictive. Being online offers the user immediate conversations and social contact. We don't have to make a physical effort; at the touch of a button, we can be engaged in conversation – it can be social, comic, political or commentary. We all exchange and can share links or our latest visual snapshot photo.

In 2018, the World Health Organisation (WHO) produced an International Classification of Diseases, which now includes those diagnosed as suffering from computer gaming addiction or gaming disorder. This means those sufferers will be entitled to be treated by the NHS[196]. It is described as:

> 'a pattern of persistent or recurrent gaming behaviour, which may be online or offline, manifested by impaired control over gaming, increasing priority given to gaming to the extent that gaming takes precedence over

---

196.https://www.telegraph.co.uk/news/2018/06/15/video-game-addicts-can-seek-treatment-nhs-condition-classified

other life interests and daily activities and continuation or escalation of gaming despite the occurrence of negative consequences.'

As in other forms of addiction (gambling, smoking, illegal or recreational drugs, paid for sex), big business and mafia often gain by protecting supply or by directly providing these services. Government, medical and social agencies attempt to mitigate the effects that addictive tendencies can create for citizens' well-being and mental health. Behavioural indicators include: significant weight gain or loss, mood changes, lack of sleep avoiding friends and family members, lying about the time spent playing, skipping meals, poor work performance, poor school attainment. Eight per cent of players report that they spend 20 hours per week playing Fortnite and similar games – this is a sign of addiction. Hard limits need to be set. Alternative activities and close supervision is advised. Applications should include technical solutions to monitor phones and restrict access.

Young people, especially teenagers, usually create their own social world in order to separate from their parents. This generation uses the term 'helicopter parenting'[197] to describe parental hovering over their children and close supervision of teenagers. Young people in this generation can be more attached to and supervised by their parents for longer than in previous generations. Often rebelling by creating their friendship groups through online communities on social media and gaming platforms, using online slang and fashion, 'friends' need re-definition. Purely online friends without any physical or social knowledge of their identities can pose a threat. Friendship is more than just 'hanging out'. Friendship facilitates the

197.https://www.parents.com/parenting/better-parenting/what-is-helicopter-parenting

development of trust, honesty, empathy and social bonding. Open discussion about what friendship may involve both online and offline, is helpful to parents and teenagers. However, children who show signs of cyber addiction should not be ignored and should be given kind, respectful and careful attention. In the first instance, subtle changes in parenting styles and family culture can overcome some challenges and prevent addictive behaviours.

However if advice fails to limit playing games and social online activities up to a maximum of ten hours a week, seek immediate help from health and social services and schools. Mumsnet offer useful advice and also point out that it is common for teenagers to deny the problem[198]. stem4[199] offers useful referral advice to help and support teenage mental health. Often computing addiction is part of a wider mental health challenge of teenager anxiety. Tackling the wider family, school and community context and challenges can help tackle the level of anxiety. Offering alternative offline social, cultural, hobbies and sport activities is crucial. Young people can extend their cyber passion into constructive, educational and career-orientated pathways by developing skills to create, design and develop computer games and digital media and culture. This will offer them a choice of careers in the Games and creative industries, such as specialist roles as a computer games coder, system designer, user experience specialist, character or environmental digital artist, computer animator or smart systems software engineer.

In April 2018, it is estimated that Fortnite made $296 million across all of its platforms (including console, PC and mobile), according to research company Superdata. This was the highest grossing

198. https://www.mumsnet.com/teenagers/teenagers-and-addiction
199. https://stem4.org.uk

digital console game that month. Fortnite Battle Royale is redefining gaming video content (GVC). In the month of May, people tuned in to watch over 574M hours of Fortnite Battle Royale content, a growth of nearly 14% from the previous month[200]. Battle Royale has quickly become one of the world's most popular and successful online multiplayer games. Its 40 million monthly users make it more popular than its giant competitor, Grand Theft Auto V Online, which is produced by Rockstar Games as part of the Grand Theft Auto franchise. These computer games are seriously profitable entertainment franchises[201].

Computer VR therapy is being used to combat mental health challenges[202]. UK organisations offer VR therapies that can help people overcome post traumatic stress disorder (PTSD). The VR solutions systematically expose the clients to previous phobias whilst controlling their level of anxiety. This is known also as graduated exposure therapy or systematic de-sensitisation therapy. Research with US veterans using VR produced the Bravemind project, a VR exposure therapy system, which provides relief from post-traumatic stress (PTS). Currently distributed to over 50 sites, including hospitals, military bases and university centres, the Bravemind system has been shown to produce a meaningful reduction in PTS symptoms[203].

200. https://www.superdataresearch.com/the-success-of-fortnite-battle-royale-is-big-enough-to-share
201. ibid
202. https://vrtherapies.co.uk and
https://www.verywellmind.com/virtual-reality-exposure-therapy-vret-2797340
203. http://medvr.ict.usc.edu/projects/bravemind

# 2.5

# Re-defining relationships online

Behavioural development is influenced by our exposure to cyber worlds. Research, today and as we evolve, is investigating these changes to reveal insights. Cybercare's insights gathered from research literature indicate that it is likely that specific personal characteristics, lowering levels of self-esteem and poor resilience impact on how people respond to cyber abuse and cyberattack.

Often women are victims, as part of a general legacy of misogyny. These traditional legacies of hate crime that have been pervasive globally in many different forms now need to be overturned. Cybercare's observations indicate that with support and advice, often victims (90% are women) increase their knowledge about how to protect themselves against cyber abuse. They, as survivors, develop resilience and a sense of empowerment. Cyber abuse is often part of the pattern of domestic abuse which can include physical and financial abuse and emotional coercion. Without education, training and awareness, gathering evidence of domestic abuse with cyber abuse (in order to enable legal enforcement and follow up) is challenging. Changes are required across the legal, social services and education systems and also guidance in terms of personal relationship expectations, to ensure people take steps to protect themselves against cyber abuse within the context of domestic abuse. New approaches to domestic trauma and abuse turn to working with family dynamics and stereotypical expectations in order to sustain long term impact. Our partners, Rise Mutual[204] with Solace Women's Aid offer joint and family based programmes.

Whilst computer gaming can be addictive, VR therapy can help people recover from trauma, phobias and anxiety disorders. Virtual worlds and platforms can bring people together who are isolated by their Otherness. Virtual online worlds enable them to locate Others like themselves.

Today, notions of romantic love, sex orientation, families and children are evolving, as they have always done. Today the internet describes this current social revolution where notions around gender stereotypes and masculinity and femininity are re-framed. Online platforms have exposed alternative genders and opened up the traditional notions of gender. It is now well accepted in medicine, psychology, social sciences and in society that the binary categories of male and female do not align with the reality that sex and gender are a continuum and may be fluid. Some people are intersex, as situated between[205]. Yet the legal system not only requires that people identify their sex status, it provides a choice of only male or female. There is no possibility of a non-specific sex. Intersex-led groups are creating online forums where intersex people are able to share their stories and meet others like them. For many individuals, this is their first opportunity

204.https://risemutual.org/2016/04/29/revealed-the-hidden-habits-that-cost-you-money
205.http://astraeafoundation.org/wearereal/#strategies-for-changemaleandfemale

to connect with another intersex person, someone who understands and can relate to their experiences. In places where geography or other factors make it difficult to meet in person, or for intersex people who don't wish to be publicly visible, online meet ups can provide an invaluable source of support[206].

Conversely, online misogyny and misandry hate crime is disseminated online through incel forums. Here, 'networked misogyny'[207] has gathered about 6,800 members. They describe themselves as sexually frustrated men who identify as involuntarily celibate (incel). They are open about their violent misogyny and encourage others to commit crimes of kidnapping, rape, incest and homicide. A similar site has been forced offline by multiple web domain registrars (e.g. Russia's RU center[208]), but it repeatedly reestablished. There are calls to combat these activities, but media commenters argue on what to do, some suggest this minority should be ignored, others attempt to deal with the underlying mental and social disorders; and government, social and legal experts advise that they should be forced off the internet as they are spreading hate crime[209].

It is reported that using the internet to call out sexual harassment and assault has been a mixed blessing for some Indian women. It has enabled and encouraged them to finally speak up; but in an arena that has not always provided the legal and moral support they need. 'People were just waiting to see who's next, with no stake, with a salacious sort of interest in this. Voyeuristic,' Rituparna Chatterjee, a journalist and

206. ibid
207. https://www.huffingtonpost.co.uk/entry/incels-cloudfare-online-content-protection
208. RU center – the largest Russian domain name registrar for business, https://www.nic.ru/en
209. 'Making misandry a hate crime will embolden abusive men', by Jessica Eaton.' It's already too easy for men to cry foul every time a woman says or does anything they don't like. Don't enshrine that in law', Wed 17 Oct 2018 08.00 BST.

activist reports. 'Meanwhile there were hundreds of women getting in touch saying, "My husband threw acid on my face", but those cases never moved forward.' The aim is to connect people to networks of lawyers and mental health professionals. An official Twitter account, @IndiaMeToo, is able to amplify stories and serve as a clearing house for information.[210] [211]

210. https://www.theguardian.com/world/2019/may/14/indias-metoo-backlash-accusers-battle-intimidation-threats-and-lawsuits
211. 'call out' – recent urban idiom - to criticize someone about something they have said or done and challenge them to explain it, 2015, Free Dictionary, Urban Dictionary

# PART 3:

# CYBER CRIME WITHIN THE GLOBAL CONTEXT

## LIVING IN A GLOBAL WORLD

None of us live on an island today, we are interconnected with the global communities in systemic interrelationships. Over 10% of Cybercare's clients have cyber threat scenarios orchestrated by alleged perpetrators who have connections with global cybercrime. We can access live maps of cyber threats produced by different cyber threat monitoring companies from Checkpoint to Kaspersky. Each of them may have different political agendas and these may be indicated on how they view and design their data feeds.

These links to live maps of cyber threats often portray a different perspective on which nation states and their agencies may be attacking and which are victims. This ongoing battle indicates attacks from many agents.

- https://threatmap.checkpoint.com/ThreatPortal/livemap.html
- https://cybermap.kaspersky.com
- http://threatbutt.com/map/
- https://www.fireeye.com/cyber-map/threat-map.html

# 3.1

# Combating Cybercrime

In order to attempt to solve cybercrime, police and law enforcement take a multiple path approach. They seek to identify the perpetrators. Global police agencies have reported that 80% of cybercrime internationally is perpetrated by four main cybercrime mafia groups. They estimate that 20% of cybercrime includes lone rangers, kiddy-hackers, non-affiliated small groups of cyber criminals.

## CRIMINALS' MOTIVATION

Police and law enforcement attempt to solve some of these crimes through a careful analysis that detects how hackers may be thinking. What does the hacker want to get out of this? What is the benefit? Who benefits? Does this crime pay better than another criminal opportunity? The reason for crime is analysed by considering motivation, opportunity, means and method. What does the criminal aim to achieve? Often their perceived reward is a combination of financial gain and power, coercive control and the fuelling of psychological factors. In some cases, psychological factors may be a complex combination of psychological disorder and sadism, i.e. socio-pathology, personality disorder, addiction and sadistic violence.

## CYBERATTACK AND CYBERCRIME: OPPORTUNITY AND TYPE

Given the 24/7 pervasive nature of online presence, there is an ongoing opportunity for criminal attack. Cyber attacks can take place anytime and anywhere by anonymous agents. In comparison, traditional crime has been limited to specific vulnerable situations, places and times. Today online criminal opportunities extend with a global reach across national jurisdictions. Online activity can easily offer unlimited access to the dark net via browsers like Tor. In addition, Bitcoin and other cryptocurrencies are used to exchange illegal goods, including contraband goods, illegal or quasi legal drugs, i.e. synthetic drugs and New Psychoactive Substances (NPS), weapons and human slavery. Internationally both state and non-state actors engage in cybercrime. Cybercrime includes: cyber warfare; espionage, cybercrime acted upon one nation state against another nation state. Cyber criminal activities require cybersecurity technical knowledge on how to hack cyber-secured IT systems.

# 3.2

# International crime linked to cybercrime

International crime linked to cybercrime covers all areas of crime. Criminals need to communicate and online tools and platforms are the most effective means of communication. Online platforms are used to enable the transportation and sale of illicit goods across national borders. Europol analysis points to trends such as: the kidnapping for ransom in Sinai of irregular migrants with EU-based sponsors in the Horn of Africa; the impact of Mexican organised criminal groups on the organised crime situation in Europe; the growing trade in counterfeit pesticides; trafficking in human beings using the internet; child trafficking for exploitation in forced criminal activities and forced begging; theft of catalytic converters.

## FINDINGS FROM EUROPOL'S EUROPEAN UNION INTERNET REFERRAL UNIT

All or many of these criminal trends make use of online activities to maximise efficiency and profit. Europol's European Union Internet Referral Unit (EU IRU), which combats terrorist propaganda and related violent extremist activities on the internet, also issues intelligence notifications. Reports on EU IRU have processed over 11,000 messages across some 31 online platforms in eight languages. The content had been put out by criminals to spread violent extremist online content material. 91.4% of the total content has been successfully removed from the platforms by the social media and online service providers.

Additionally, EU IRU has expanded its open-source and internet monitoring activities in order to contribute to the disruption of illegal migrant smuggling networks. Content advertising smuggling services for migrants and refugees is referred so it can be removed. EU IRU is working with online service companies to promote 'self-regulation' activities by the online industry.

## EUROPE – EU – WORKING TOGETHER TO COMBAT CYBERCRIME

EMPACT[212] is a structured multidisciplinary co-operation platform of the relevant Member States, EU institutions and agencies, as well as third countries, international organisations and other (public and private) partners to address the prioritised threats of organised and serious international crime. Their focus is cybercrime, drug trafficking, illegal immigration, organised property crime, human trafficking, missing trader MTIC fraud, illicit weapons and arms, environmental crime and illicit waste trafficking, money laundering and fraudulent documents[213]. Whilst Europe describes their fight against cybercrime as indicated below, all the other

212. https://www.europol.europa.eu/empact
213. https://www.europol.europa.eu/crime-areas-and-trends/crime-areas/economic crime/mtic-missing-trader-intra-community-fraud. Costing revenue authorities around EUR 60 billion annually in tax losses, missing trader intra-community (MTIC) fraud is the theft of value-added tax (VAT) from a government by organised crime groups. VAT fraud us a highly complex form of tax fraud that relies on the abuse of the VAT rules for cross-border transactions.

criminal activities also use online communication channels and platforms.

Europol's first challenge is to (1) disrupt the criminal activities related to attacks against information systems, particularly those following a Crime-as-a-Service business model and working as enablers for online crime, (2) combat child sexual abuse and child sexual exploitation, including the production and dissemination of child abuse material, and (3) target criminals involved in fraud and counterfeiting of non-cash means of payment, including large-scale payment card fraud (especially card-not-present fraud), emerging threats to other non-cash means of payment and enabling criminal activities.

Online criminal activities include trends in[214]: illegal trafficking of people, drugs, weapons, illicit goods, fraud, blackmail, human slavery, corporate fraud, targeted cyber abuse towards specific individuals and families, general scattergun type scams, targeted malicious attacks to individuals by individuals, hacking, copyright infringement, illegal mass-surveillance, child pornography, grooming and terrorism.

Cyberspace can be used to terrorise people or a nation; to enable terrorists to promote terrorist propaganda and to raise funds to finance their terrorist activities. The pervasive cyber world and its online communication networks are used for legal and illegal purposes be it international travel or international funds transfer or global communication.

---

214. https://www.europol.europa.eu/crime-areas-and-trends/crime-areas/trafficking-in-human-beings

# 3.3

# Why does global cybercrime work?

Cybercrime is scaleable, anonymous, and aggregated. Cybercrime can reach many people; many phishing emails may be sent and the hackers may get lucky with a few people who have a lack of cyber awareness. Cybercrime is global, reaching across national jurisdictions. A computer virus or downloading site could be located elsewhere from the criminal activity that it may be responsible for, so it is difficult to trace. Cybercrime can be large scale, anonymous, their profit aggregated for substantial return. Large scale databases of compromised emails and personal data are available on the Dark Net. An example of a scaled, anonymous, aggregated method is a botnet sending out masses of phishing emails and ransomware, intending to blackmail victims. We can carry out checks to note the status of any email address. Are our emails clean or compromised and for sale on the Dark Net?

The modus operandi of the perpetrators and criminals varies and is hard to find the perpetrator. Usually the cybercrime is operational orchestrated from a remote location. In most cases, it might be from a different country. The perpetrator may use technical knowledge such as VPNs or hidden proxies to avoid digital footprint and detection.

## WHO ARE THE TARGETED VICTIMS AND WHO ARE THE PERPETRATORS?

Targeted victims are divided into two main categories:

1. Computer as a target: Crimes that primarily target computer networks or devices (viruses, DDOS attacks, malware).
2. Individuals as a target: in cases of crime against individuals, the computer may only be used as a tool (scams, theft, stalking, fraud, identity theft).

Our vulnerability to cybercrime is directly proportional to our reliance on the internet in our modern lifestyle. Using mobile phones we are connected to cyber space due to the convenience that it offers. Lack of awareness and ability to configure our IT systems and internet-enabled products make some of us more vulnerable.

## CHALLENGES WITH CYBERCRIME EVIDENCE

As mentioned before, there is a real challenge to gather evidence of cybercrime. These are due to:

- Online crime is a variant of other crimes (blackmail, bullying, fraud, theft, violence and abuse).
- Online evidence is maybe indirect, circumstantial and is linked with other evidence of offline criminal activities.
- Under-reporting and inconsistencies.

- Lack of clarity around the government Cybersecurity Strategy (see below).
- Evidence from industry is not transparent, and is likely to be influenced by vested interests/commercial bias.
- Lack of standardisation, measures and comparability. For example, naming conventions for malware, descriptions of online criminal activity, units of measurements. ('I think what tends to work well is transparency, which I think is an area where we need to do a lot better and are working on', says Facebook's CEO Mark Zuckerberg.)
- Lack of design heuristics and design codes to secure IoT products. In response to the threat of IoT products, the UK Government published in February 2019, *The Government's Code of Practice for Consumers* (IoT Security for manufacturers, with guidance for consumers on smart devices at home. https://www.gov.uk/government/collections/secure-by-design, authored by David Rogers of Copper Horse.
- Under representation of vulnerable communities, for example, domestic abuse victims, the elderly, human trafficking, slavery victims, children and other vulnerable groups.
- Procedures and methods of law enforcement. Procedures around gathering evidence. For example the difficulties in the collection and presentation of online crime in cases of domestic abuse and coercion as noted in our services at Cybercare UK.
- Distinction between lack of basic IT skills including cyber hygiene and IT hacking and intrusion by malicious perpetrators.

# 3.4

# Strategy needs clarity, resilience and long-term planning

UK National Cyber Security Strategy needs clearer long-term objectives built on a firmer evidential basis, according to a new report from the Public Accounts Committee. The strategy, which covers the five-year period from 2016 to 2021, has been 'hampered by a weak evidence base and lack of business case'[215].

All areas in the UK are seen to be tackling the cyber threat[216]. The UK Government reports that 'the UK is particularly vulnerable to the risk of cyberattacks'. In light of this, the committee recommends that the Cabinet Office ensures that another long-term plan for cybersecurity in the UK is in place long before the March 2021 end date of the existing strategy. MPs also concluded that the department 'cannot justify how its approach to cybersecurity is delivering value for money'. To remedy this, the Cabinet Office must make sure any further long-term plans for cybersecurity are supported by 'a properly costed business case'.

---

215. https://www.holyrood.com/articles/news/uk-national-cyber-security-strategy-needs-clearer-long-term-objectives-says-public
216. https://www.holyrood.com/articles/news/public-sector-workers-be-given-cyber-resilience-toolkit-better-help-business

Central government agency also 'lacks the robust evidence base it needs to make informed decisions about cybersecurity', the report concluded. MPs had requested that the Cabinet Office set out to show what progress it is making in using evidence-based decisions in prioritising cybersecurity work. The MPs asked that: 'This should include plans for undertaking a robust "lessons learnt" exercise to capture all relevant evidence from the current strategy and programme to support any future approach to cybersecurity'. The penultimate conclusion of the report is that 'the department has not been clear what the strategy will actually deliver by 2021'. MPs recommend that the Cabinet Office publishes in Autumn 2019 a clear set of goals for what the strategy should deliver, as well as 'the risks around those areas where it will not meet its strategic outcomes and objectives'.

Finally, concluding that 'government has not yet done enough to enhance cybersecurity throughout the economy and better protect consumers'. In remediation, the Cabinet Office is asked to write to the committee sometime in the next five months 'outlining how it intends to influence the different sectors in the economy... to provide consumers with information on their cyber resilience'. Additionally, the committee said that the post-2021 cybersecurity strategy should include plans for how best to protect consumers.

Committee chair Meg Hillier said:

> 'We welcome the National Cyber Security Strategy but are concerned that the programme designed to deliver it is insufficient. As it currently stands, the strategy is not supported by the robust evidence the department needs to make informed decisions and accurately measure progress. On top of this, neither the

strategy or the programme were grounded in business cases – despite being allocated £1.9bn funding.'

Hillier added:

'Looking longer term, we are disappointed that the department was not able to give us a clear idea of what the strategy will deliver by 2021. This does not represent a resilient security strategy. In the interest of national security, the Cabinet Office need to take a long-term approach to protecting against the risk of cyberattacks: future plans should be based on strong evidence, business cases should be rigorously costed to ensure value for money, and strategic outcomes and objectives should be clearly defined.[217]'

Whilst their recommendations are commendable, outlining how they intend to influence the different sectors in the economy—for example, retail—to provide consumers with information on their cyber resilience and how to measure success in protecting consumers in order to approach to deal with the challenges of cybersecurity after 2021, they also need to address the life-long education and thereby protection of citizens, individuals, families, communities, the vulnerable and the digitally reluctant.

## IS DEMOCRACY SAFE?

The British government's Houses of Parliament use Microsoft Sharepoint; what is the evidence that this

217. https://www.parliament.uk/business/committees/committees-a-z/commons-select/public-accounts-committee/news-parliament-2017/cyber-security-in-the-uk-report-published-17-19

US based international corporate collaborative IT system offers the most secure IT system appropriate for MPs and senior civil staff responsible for the UK Government? The new Cloud data bill[218] from the US enables the international legal framework to access data stored in remote servers outside of the US. The US Government is reportedly using Amazon and Google cloud servers and services. Do these corporate collaborative IT systems offer the most secure systems appropriate for people responsible for government? Are the tech giants or other nation states in control?

218. https://www.diplomacy.edu/blog/us-cloud-act-implications-and-reactions
https://data-economy.com/while-you-were-busy-with-gdpr-the-us cloud-act-was-passed-and-it-has-significant impact-for-european-organisations

# 3.5

# International corporate
# cyber threats

The World Economic Forum indicates that it is the interconnectivity between political unrest in conflict areas, environmental threat and cybercrime that could lead to exponential increase, sudden paradigmatic shifts or 'radical and irreversible systemic shocks'[219].

There is a rise in cyber breaches, the use of the dark net to traffic illegal weapons, drugs and cryptocurrency and massive data fraud. Cyber targets are increasing, as people and organisations access the internet of things – IOT. These threats are constantly evolving and include DDOS, WannaCry, Petya and NotPetya, spear-phishing attacks (stealing data or installing malware using individually targeted email scams).

Often the cyber attack includes a combination of 'intruder threat' and social behaviour manipulation, known as social engineering. In some of these scams, a human may need to click the malicious link on an email or website or install what looks like official known software updates. It is very easy for a computer savvy

219. 'Global Risks 2018: Fractures, Fears and Failures' (Weforum, 2018) http://reports.weforum.org/global-risks-2018/global-risks-2018-fractures-fears-and-failures

individual hacker to send an email or social media text to a potential victim with a coded link, that when clicked, will give the hacker remote access to the victim's email or social media account.

Corporate cybercrimes include blackmail using ransomware; espionage gaining remote access to reveal company secrets; threat and blackmail using Malware: every three seconds a company is infected with Malware. It can take up to 90 days to detect a breach.

Cyber fraud occurs across national barriers as the internet is a global network. Cyber fraud is pervasive and prevalent across all sectors of society; from individual access to a corporate online system or physical entry, to identity fraud to dating scams to swindle a victim's money.

In order to tackle cybercrime across national borders, legal enablers used to gain access to evidence to support law enforcement. In the US, the CLOUD Act was introduced to address the situations where the FBI wanted to obtain remote data through service providers, e.g. to investigate a 2013 drug trafficking case. Here, emails from a US citizen on one of Microsoft's remote servers in Ireland were required as evidence. The legal challenge led to the Supreme Court in the case Microsoft Corp. v. United States[220]. Moreover, there could be potential conflict between GDPR and the CLOUD Act[221]. Pearse-Trust clarifies: 'The CLOUD Act means that US law enforcement can demand data and emails to be handed over if stored by a US company, regardless of where in the world the data is stored. This has serious implications for EU organisations using public cloud services. In contrast, the EU's GDPR situates itself at the opposite end of the

220. https://caselaw.findlaw.com/us-dc-circuit/1436071.html
221. https://www.reedsmith.com/en/perspectives/2018/06/potential-conflict-and-harmony-between-gdpr-and-the-cloud-act

spectrum, putting individual privacy rights ahead of law enforcement needs, in order to protect the personal data of EU citizens.[222]'

In UK, Norwich Pharmacal orders (NPOs) are commonly sought against ISPs in order to compel disclosure of information held by them about their user. The principle originates from the House of Lords case, *Norwich Pharmacal Co v Customs and Excise Commissioners* (1974)[223] 'There have been a number of NPO applications made to the High Court to identify fraudsters on the internet, often "trolls" or fraudsters. Once identified, it is not possible to hide behind a virtual identity and the individuals can be prosecuted for offences such as fraud or harassment[224].' However, other legal opinion[225] deduces that 'a Norwich Pharmacal order cannot be used to order the provision of evidence for foreign proceedings, regardless of whether the foreign jurisdiction provides a mechanism for obtaining such evidence via the statutory regime'[226]. In conversation with UK lawyers, it has been pointed out that the UK's NPO is not fit for this purpose and may be superseded by GDPR and other digital data legislation. The implications of the EU's GDPR points the way to a privileging of the rights of the individual to retain the privacy of personal data privacy as opposed to the interests of US law enforcement having jurisdiction over all data held by US companies.

222. https://www.pearse-trust.ie/blog/the-us-cloud-act-v-the-eus-gdpr-data-privacy-security
223. Sjovoll, [Accessed 31st March 2019] https://inforrm.org/2017/10/26/online-publication-claims-norwich-pharmacal-orders-and-jurisdiction-issues-kirsten-sjovoll/
224. McMahon, Sandberg [Accessed 31st March 2019] https://www.emmlegal.com/news/norwich-pharmacal-order-npo
225. Smith Freehills, 2012.
226. Smith Freehills, 2012, www.lexology.com

## NATIONAL, LOCAL, TECH GIANTS AND SUPERPOWERS

Digital sovereignty of nation states ensures the security of territorial borders. This, in turn, maintains revenue and tax that feeds the national economic benefit. Today, this is perceived to be under threat, where the economic power of the national state may be superseded by the digital technology giants, or a greater alliance of other nation states or superpowers. It is this power struggle which is now being played out online, and through technical, legal and physical networks.

## TECHNICAL AND LEGAL METHODS TO MAINTAIN TERRITORIAL BORDERS[227]

To ensure digital sovereignty, various methods are proposed to ensure territorial borders on the Internet. In some cases, these methods seek to retain economic benefits for local regions, or to impose socio-cultural regimes.

Some examples of this are:

1.  Nigerian laws, which impose 'data localisation' requirements to open local offices and data centres[228].
2.  Blocking of URLs (uniform resource locators) and blocking of Internet protocol (IP) addresses via the national Internet service providers (ISP).

227. https://www.internetjurisdiction.net/uploads/pdfs/Articles/20161014-ORF-PDF.pdf
https://www.ilincnetwork.eu/wp-content/uploads/2015/08/3-LB-The-Limited-Liability-of-Internet-Intermediaries-in-the-EU-Update.docx.pdf
https://www.ilincnetwork.eu/
http://ec.europa.eu/priorities/digital-single- market/docs/dsm-communica-tion_en.pdf
228. Ahilari, Abuja 2017, Punch; InfoSec Nigeria-UK Trade Industry seminar February 2019

3.   The demand for backdoors to encryption technologies by Nation States.
4.   The imposition of intermediary liability regimes and full-fledged licensing regimes. Liability regimes insist on methods to define reasonable care and how to distinguish Internet services, which can act alternatively or as well as a conduit, as a cache, and a host.

## TACKING CYBERCRIME ACROSS THE GLOBE

Corporate cyber attacks in the private sector have a major impact on government operations and society. In order to tackle cybercrime, how can cross-border access to e-evidence be enabled but at the same time, respect and maintain the privacy of the individual? On the global level, investigations and resources are being identified by: the World Economic Forum, Interpol, with the UK leading on promoting standards for cyber security IoT product design.

European and Global directives have created a programme of events and directives to achieve a value-driven agenda promoted by EU, WEF, and DAVOS. Meanwhile different global powers are re-aligning their alliances and stimulating trade wars set against the background of crypto-currencies[229] offering new methods of exchange cultures and that could undermine current traditional currencies. There is an argument that the banks are a lot more sceptical about the benefit of cryptocurrencies than is made out in the media[230].

However banks are already experimenting with blockchain. Blockchain may radically alter the way banking is done and if so the banks as expert major

229. Cryptocurrencies use blockchain technology. This is an open, distributed ledger that can record transactions between two parties efficiently and in a verifiable and permanent way.
230. https://decrypt.co/4189/institional-investors-crypto-fact

institutions want to be ahead of the game[231]. Albanian gangs are laundering their funds using cryptocurrencies as reported by Britain's leading organised crime officer, Peter Goodman[232].

Within the USA, despite the current Trumpism of 'for America only', there is a rising democratic lobby advocating for our cyber futures to be embedded with humanistic values, for example, Ray Kurzweil and the SU and Ramesh Srinivasan of UCLA. Within China and its expansionist vision for its infrastructure and world dominance, there is a vision and assertive promotion of a no-tariff, no-tax free trade digital highway. Within Africa, there is a hunger for 5G and broadband infrastructure but with a demand for localisation of data centres and self-governing control.

## PROGRAMME OF EUROPEAN AND GLOBAL DIRECTIVES 2002 – 2020

2002 European level: Universal service obligations and users' rights are identified by Directive 2002/22/EC of the European Parliament and of the Council (Universal Service Directive)

2017 UK: Balance between market flexibility and legal regulation to ensure the protection of services for the individuals, SMES and communities. http://www.legislation.gov.uk/ukpga/2017/30/contents/enacted/data.htm

2018: WEF created a consortium of financial services and technology companies to help protect the growing financial technology ('fintech') industry and its customers from cyber security threats. Last year's cyberattacks damaged private sector computers, but they also

---

231. https://www.accountingsuite.com/cryptocurrencies
232. August 2019, https://www.thetimes.co.uk/edition/news/albanian-gangs-using-bitcoin-to-flood-streets-with-cocaine-7j70j6z7l

impacted the operation of government, and had knock-on effects for society and the economy.

2019 EU: The Council discussed the negotiating mandates for the second Additional Protocol to the Budapest Convention on Cybercrime 2001. This international treaty on cybercrime, seeks to harmonise national laws, improve investigative techniques, and increase cooperation among nations. These mandates would complement the EU e-evidence legislative package. In March 2019, 63 states ratified the Budapest convention, while a further four states had signed the convention but not ratified it.

2020 Cyber Futures conference at Davos, January 21st:

1. Systemic cyber threats and resilience
2. Standardisation of cyber education globally
3. Measures of Cyber Risk – qualification, quantification and mitigation
4. Bringing cyber criminals to justice
5. Mistrust through dissemination of fake news and influence
6. Corporate cyber programs:
   http://cyberfuturedialogue.org

# PART 4:
# THE HERE AND NOW

# 4.1

# Surveillance, geo locators, we are being watched

Citizens are being watched in detail, everywhere, 24/7. What does this mean? Is it true? Why and what are the benefits and dangers?[233] Beam reports that satellites that give us Google Earth details and visual data are being used by law enforcement agencies to view illegal activities of citizens, from the illegal growing of marijuana, to detecting illegal abuse of the environment. Human rights activists have used satellite imagery technology to identify that the Chinese Government have misled the western media, by describing their detention camps for the Urghur minority as 'vocational schools'.

Satellite images are becoming sharper and taken more frequently. Today, there are 768 in orbit. Global legal regulatory frameworks need to ensure ethical values and guidance for technology controls to protect privacy and freedom, but also to benefit law enforcement and human rights. The technology improves exponentially to produce sharper and clearer

---

233. 2019, Christopher Beam https://www.technologyreview.com/s/613748/satellites-threaten-privacy

images. Beam reports that US federal regulations limit images taken by commercial satellites to a resolution of 25 cm, or about the length of a man's shoe in order to ensure some anonymity for citizens. Sharper image resolution is kept for military and classified use.

Helicopters and low flying planes are used by law enforcement agencies on a regular basis, combining visualisation tools and heat sensors to monitor and track crime. In the UK, the London Metropolitan Police employ surveillance technology to ensure the safety of Londoners and detect criminality[234].

We are players within this surveillance culture. The culture of being watched and followed and watching others has been created by pervasive satellite surveillance and the geo-locators prevalent on all smartphones, browsers and applications unless turned off.

'net.art', with its many artists and thinkers, comment on and critique this surveillance and how the use of these technologies is changing our lifestyles, sense of self and our human right to privacy and freedom[235]. In a benign world, where liberal values are espoused, the law protects the individual and minorities from the tyranny of the majority. One might view this surveillance as necessary to ensure cyber-citizens' safety from terrorism, infringements against the environmental good, ensuring human rights for freedom of thought and self-determination, education, water and resources, food, computer literacy and cybersecurity.

Government or powerful forces in any region may offer a compassionate model of society to its citizens. This may be a benign liberal democracy or social democracy, for example, the European model; or other

234. https://www.standard.co.uk/news/london/mystery-plane-circles-london-sparking-surveillance-rumours-9623518.html
235. https://www.net-art.org/surveillance-camera-players

types of democracies which offer education for all, or a compassionate semi-authoritarian state which aims to offer education for all, for example, Egypt or Jordan.

Today these surveillance tools may be used and perceived to be protecting the people within a wide range of relatively benign nation states. However, with a fascist and authoritarian regime in control, this surveillance technology and culture can easily be used against the citizens as an effective tool for intimidation, threat and suppression, turning benign nation states into fascistic regimes.

Our western societies and others are built around the values of the Enlightenment, offering governments supported and created by an educated populace that appreciates and seeks to gain knowledge from the discoveries of science and reason and works to emulate humanistic values. Cognitive science and networked computer technologies are capable of working with our data in order to maximise good health, prosperity, safety, peace, and mental health. Education on the ethical implications and use of emerging advent technologies and their effective regulatory frameworks is essential. This education enables us as cyber-citizens to proactively engage with these challenges to achieve the best use of this surveillance technology.

# 4.2

# Cyber learning and education

Today, society has a skills deficit in IT, computing and technology. Government and educational directives seek to address this gap. Enabling a workforce to create and use technology in itself is not a 'cure'. Working in technology, experts have recognised the need for a multi-disciplinary and complex system approach. We must collaborate with the users and stake-holder groups to understand the users' psychological requirements, the logistics and complexity of any system to fine tune the technology's effectiveness and efficacy. Skills delivered by humanities, arts and physical activities are essential to understand how users can navigate through systems, communicate, build conceptual maps, use stories as communication vehicles and physically engage in augmented, embedded, or virtual 3D environments.

Each year at London Tech Week, related conferences and trade shows showcase dynamic start-ups and new applications at their beta stage of delivery and ready for market technology products. Niki Chesworth[236] reports two in three companies have unfilled digital vacancies. Digital skills needs are set to rocket across

236. Niki Chesworth, 'Think a tech role isn't for you?' Evening Standard, 10th June 2019.

industries: 'UK is losing out on £63 billion a year as companies struggle to find people with the right digital skills.' The public sector is employing graduates to move into technical roles in order to deliver smart systems and AI to ensure an effective public service. Job roles include Robotic Integration Developer, whose role is to develop and use smart systems, for example developing a call reminder system that picks up cancelations automatically freeing up appointments to be booked for other patients, or automated systems to streamline GP referrals. There is government funding for IT start-ups, innovation hubs and accelerator networks, for example, Innovate, Digital Catapult and the Knowledge Transfer Network. Other professional networks focus on specific technologies: MeetUps[237] and forums, including the Institute of Engineering and Electronics (IEE)[238]; BCS British Computer Society, renamed as BCS, the Chartered Institute for IT[239]; Women in Telecoms and Technology (WiTT)[240] and Animated Women UK (AWUK)[241]. Traditionally, IT and technology has been male dominated but now aims to appeal to a diverse demographic.

Higher Education in Computing and Computer Science was mostly split into specialist areas of Computer Science, Computing, Electronic Engineering and Mathematics. Today, industry requirements have radically changed, demanding skills in smart systems using Computer Vision, Machine Learning and AI, Data Science, Communication Networking with Security, User Experience and Embedded Technology creating wearable or transplanted computing and virtual, augmented and immersive realities. The future is here as medical computerised devices are embedded into our

237. https://www.meetup.com
238. https://www.theiet.org
239. https://www.bcs.org
240. http://www.wittgroup.org
241. http://www.animatedwomenuk.com

physical bodies. The human body is becoming the next computer interface[242].

Computerised devices are being designed to obtain more sensitive readings than our human sensor interface, feeding into smart intelligent systems, an increase of complex data. Gestural interfaces are being designed to be triggered using micro gestures. Advances in research and development into DNA, nanobots and synthetic biology could be integrated to offer accelerated skill learning and multi-disciplinary intelligences. Educational frameworks will need radical transformation to accommodate the educational requirements of the cyborg generation.

The EVA[243] conference is one example of influential globally networked interdisciplinary forums that bring together innovative research and development concerning arts, visualisations and IT including 3D environments and animation, AI, heritage, museums, philosophy, social media, innovative audio and VR.

Education on all its tiers across all life stages, is now online or becoming online. Some training is now immersive and will become the new standard platform for health and medicine, engineering and construction. Online education is not exclusively online, but a blended mix of online virtual and immersion, blended with face-to-face people skills and some of which might remain physical where that traditional method offers real benefits. Learning needs to be 'life-long learning' as we adapt to the evolving environments and create career portfolios. Cultural and community lifestyles will be encouraged to sustain an engaged and settled population while robotics and automation take over many traditional roles.

---

242. https://www.fastcompany.com/1671960/why-the-human-body-will-be-the-next-computer-interface
243. http://www.eva-london.org

# 4.3

# Information warfare and online disinformation

Fake News encourages us to ask: What is truth? The nature of objectivity as shared truths that shift determined by changes in values and systems of belief. Unpicking the truth to lay bare ideologically assumed values. The 'trumped up' version of truths can be seen to be perpetuated by streams of false and opinionated tweets disseminated across social media. Specific social media feeds generated by famous personalities can be received by any citizen who is a social media consumer. Individual consumers choose to receive these channels. The content is then easily extracted by journalists and then they choose to publish these notable extracts through traditional broadcast media channels. On social media, a citizen has a choice to add or remove any specific feed such as a politician's channel to on one's own social media feed. As citizens, we might feel free not to receive specific social media messages; however, we are fed advertising feeds in response to our personalised search data or our personal profiles.

Often, while browsing for one type of information, quite another type of information is displayed. Spurious websites perpetuated by extremists can be revealed in error when a browser search is mis-targeted. It is as if walking in a city, one turns down a hidden alley into unfamiliar streets with very different values, struggles and sensibilities. The search engines within the browser uses the meta tagging of specific search words and their combined probabilities to reveal previously undiscovered online pages and worlds. As citizen-consumer, we make an assessment and can decide to turn away and explore elsewhere or we can follow our curiosity. Exploring the Internet safely requires us to make a critical and supported assessment of what to search for and what to reject as false and or not beneficial or valuable to our lives. We might use technical solutions and products that activate filters, parental control, and other methods to black-list these un-wanted links. However, that it is not the default position for individuals. We need to choose to reject and avoid.

Faced with the multiple world views and types of truths represented online, the capability to assess validity, authenticity, probability and how to identify what may be truth, is critical. Does this exclude citizens, who may find it challenging to grasp probabilistic and analytical thinking?[244] In the TV dystopian drama *Years and Years*[245], the character Viv, the fascist populist politician, proposes that the vote should only be extended to those with an IQ of 70 and over. This seems to respond to citizens' popular frustration, who perceive a seemingly lack of analytical competencies in society. Yet this fascist attitude threatens the democratic rights embedded in the notion of Universal Suffrage. Today, we understand IQ as a construction that measures a range of competencies and does not necessarily include

244. https://www.amanet.org/articles/companies-see-need-to-build-analyti-cal-skills-in-their-organizations-a
245. Years and Years, 2019, https://www.bbc.co.uk/programmes/m000539g

practical or creative thinking. IQ in itself may not be a true predictor of successful life skills. In an employer's report for the government in 2017[246], it was noted that there is a deficit in analytical skills. There is an ever increasing need for citizens to understand concepts around probabilistic understanding, paradigms of science and the influence of magical thinking. Centuries before, people struggled with concepts of cause and effect, choosing to worship stone inanimate objects and believe in superstition. Today, we struggle with making choices based on probabilistic thinking and the nature of 'evidence'. The reality is that life experiences have never been so good for the majority of people, most of the time. However, given the bombardment and dominance of sensational media, bad news and fake news coverage, people can be overly pessimistic, anxious and depressed. The cyber world offers both risks and benefits. Our cyberselves now have many opportunities for engagement with communities, education and ethics.

246. Employers Skills Survey 2017, https://assets.publishing.service.gov.uk/government/uploads/system/uploads/attachment_data/file/746493/ESS_2017_UK_Report_Controlled  v06.00.pdf

# PART 5

# THE FUTURE

## CYBERSELVES

We are now cyberselves; many of us have online identities or avatars, with digital implants we become cyborgs and we are becoming transhuman. Through digital culture and communities we are enhancing our lifestyles, sharing our value systems and exchanging culture. These experiences need to be regulated to ensure the balance between our individual privacy and security. Processes of regulation and protection need to be on-going, taking into account many stakeholders, locally and globally. There is not one end goal, but a process of becoming and evolving. Physical touch, rapport and empathy are crucial so we do not become detached from our humanity and humanistic values. Care is needed to educate and nurture the digitally reluctant and cautious to avoid a digital divide.

## BECOMING DIGITAL

As we incorporate digital assistants and robots into our cyber lifestyles, we remember that humans have designed help-mates, daemons and golems throughout our cultural myths and legends, as far back as Enkidu – the wild man and Gilgamesh – the civilised man. These stories help us understand our evolution. We are evolving as we design and develop our environment, whether as hunter, gatherer, knowledge worker, data analyst or eco-warrior.

## CYBER BENEFITS

Smart systems with their AI functions need to incorporate ethics and understanding of users' experience into the heart of their design. Cryptocurrencies could move away from being associated with criminal activities towards addressing and challenging cybercrime and financial exclusion.

Our cyber lifestyle offers new opportunities for designers, artists, influencers and communities. Technologies can be used for good, perpetuating a value-driven agenda, and bringing communities of interest together. Immersive platforms offer new intense experiences, and enhance seepage from the virtual to the real. What happens online matters and is directly integrated with our physical real world.

## CYBER RISKS AND BALANCES

Alongside the benefits of our cyber world, there is the growing threat of cybercrime. This needs to be tackled local, nationally and globally. Strategies from nation states, superpowers, alliances and technology giants need to be joined up, collaborative, clear and resilient. These political powers need to service the social needs of their populations, through positive engagement and listening carefully at the local level.

Children, those who may be vulnerable, and all individuals need protection from cyber addiction, cyber theft and cyber abuse. Values of trust, respect and an enabling of diversity and difference need to lead our educational and strategic agenda. Children, families and communities need to be protected.

The delicate balance between our personal freedom and our security is determined by regulatory frameworks around global surveillance technologies and operations. We all need to understand the processes that can achieve these checks and balances and how we can contribute to this crucial decision-making.

## CYBER, YOU, EDUCATION AND ETHICS

Education in cyber technologies within multi-disciplinary portfolios, across all tiers and life-long is essential for empowerment of individuals, communities and democratic systems. The nature of 'truth' and 'evidence' is a crucial ethical and philosophical investigation which is as relevant today as in our past. As cyber-enhanced humans, we should be free to choose to create and demand justice, compassion and truth, both online and offline.

# Acknowledgments

Kez Garner, co-Director of Cybercare Ltd; Cybercare Ltd, Cybercare Trust and Dreamstudio.io teams for their commitment and personal investment into our collaborative research and development, services, products and communities which we have been designing and building together.

Cybercare and DreamStudio.io partners, customers and clients whose responses feed forward into the development of our approach and services.

Ruth Cigman - for all our conversations on ethics and philosophy, life and deep friendship.

Judith Elkan, Maria Canete and Arturo Ezquerro – for their insights on Attachment theories and the Psychological.

Mehmet Mulla – for his insights as a user experience specialist and colleague.

Dr Nick Lambert, Head of Research at Ravensbourne University and Professor Karim Ouazzane, founder of Cyber Security Research Centre at London Metropolitan University for their knowledge and support.

Danny Allen, my husband, for his clarity, kindness, patience, sense of humour and endless support. To our six children for their cyber insights. Max and Cecile Elstein, my parents, for their first draft reading and encouragement. To all my family, friends and colleagues, for our interesting conversations, insights and reflections on this evolving world and the embracing of Cyber into our lives.

Legend Publishing team: Liza Paderes for her patience, support and imagination to suggest and encourage this book. Imran Mirza, Ditte Loekkegaard and Heloise Chalmers for their editing.